Feel Better Now

FEEL BETTER NOW

30 Ways to Handle Frustration in Three Minutes or Less

By Dr. Christan Schriner

Foreword by Ken Keyes, Jr.
Author of *Handbook to Higher Consciousness*

JALMAR PRESS
Rolling Hills Estates, California

Library of Congress Cataloging-in-Publication Data

Schriner, Christan, 1943-
   Feel better now: 30 ways to handle frustration in three minutes or less / by Christan Schriner; foreword by Ken Keyes, Jr.
      p.   cm.
   Includes bibliographical references.
   ISBN 0-915190-66-4 : $9.95
   1. Stress (Psychology)   2. Stress management.   3. Frustration.
I. Title.
BF575.S73S36   1990   90-31680
155.9′042—dc20   CIP

The stories and examples in this book are based upon real events, but names and circumstances have been altered to protect privacy.

Published by Jalmar Press
45 Hitching Post Drive
Rolling Hills Estates, California 90274
Tel: (213) 547-1240

First edition
Printing   10 9 8 7 6 5 4 3 2 1

Dedication

To the one who listened, Carl Rogers
and the one who challenged, Fritz Perls

Acknowledgements

Many people have offered me advice and encouragement about this book. I can mention only a few of those whose assistance was most essential. Dr. William R. Parker's kind words helped me continue to focus on the project, even when there seemed to be no time for it. Dr. Robert Schuller and Ken Keyes provided comments on the manuscript for which I will always be grateful. My office assistant, Clover Behrend, was thorough and conscientious. I was also glad for the support of my friend, Ken Lane, and my literary agent, Michael Larsen.

This book draws upon a rich variety of psychological and spiritual traditions. Early in my work as a therapist, I began looking for shortcuts in coping with pressure situations—ways of handling anxiety, stress, and conflict in a matter of moments. I found valuable ideas in my study of guided imagery, gestalt therapy, kundalini yoga, massage, creative movement, psychodrama, Living Love, the Sedona Method, the Silva Method, and Re-Evaluation Counseling. I have streamlined techniques from these disciplines to develop strategies that work most rapidly and directly.

Finally, I want to thank the many men and women who took part in my letting go workshops, as early as 1976. Their feedback convinced me that no single stress reduction technique could fit every problem and every personality. Instead of one technique, my students wanted to learn a variety of different tactics for quickly handling frustrations. I tried to locate books that offered such rapid-release techniques, but none were available. *Feel Better Now* was written to fill this void.

Contents

Foreword

One thing I appreciate about this book is that it's a highly practical, usable resource. Chris explains his ideas and techniques very clearly. He also provides numerous examples so we can see how to apply these principles in everyday living.

The main theme of *Feel Better Now* is what Chris calls "letting go." Most of us realize that letting go of tension is a key to happiness, health, and productivity. This book explains the dynamics of letting go in illuminating detail—how it feels, how we block it, and how we can allow it to happen. Chris' methods are very specific and they work rapidly.

Besides explaining the process of letting go, *Feel Better Now* also provides a number of valuable bonuses. There's an entire chapter on why we unconsciously resist feeling good. Another chapter deals with pleasure-anxiety, the nagging discomfort many people experience when they really start enjoying themselves. Chapter Fourteen provides excellent suggestions for taking the tug-of-war feeling out of a close relationship. Chris even includes a section on the pitfalls and limitations of his own methods. *Feel Better Now* is a solid, honest book. Its value will stand the test of time.

Ken Keyes, Jr., Author of
Handbook to Higher Consciousness

Feeling Good and Doing Fine

Recently I offered three hours of counseling at a fund-raising auction for charity. The two highest bidders wrote their checks to the charity, and I scheduled stress management sessions with each of them. Ironically both of them canceled their sessions before the first meeting. They were afraid that finding time for the appointments would *add* more stress than the counseling sessions would alleviate!

I understand their predicament. In the most tension-packed era of history, people don't have time to relax. Part of the problem is that most relaxation techniques take too long to use in the middle of a crisis. When the boss blows up or the radiator boils over, we can't just wander off and meditate under a tree. *The ability to cope with tension in minutes or even seconds is a basic requirement for emotional survival and physical health.* Fortunately it's a skill that we all can learn.

If we don't neutralize our upsets as soon as they arise, a number of symptoms begin to appear. Which of these symptoms have you experienced?

1. I work hard to get everything done, but my chores are never finished. I'm always pushing to catch up.
2. I feel tight places in my body, and when I glance at myself in the mirror, I see strain and physical tension.
3. Work is stressful, or boring, or both.
4. I battle with bad habits, such as smoking, overeating, or overspending.
5. I'm haunted by regrets from the past, and worries about the future.
6. I need alcohol or sleeping pills to unwind after a rough day.

7. It's hard to cut loose and have fun.
8. The world changes so fast it makes my head spin! I wish everything would hold still for a while.
9. I love my family and friends, but being with them is often dull or disagreeable.
10. I've made some real gains in my life, but I seldom feel proud of myself.

There's good news and bad news about this list. The bad news is that most people identify with at least half of these items. The good news is that by using some very specific techniques we can feel better whenever we have a few minutes of cool-off time. We can relax and calm down while driving to work, making a routine phone call, picking up groceries, shaving, showering, applying makeup, or feeding the cat. We can turn these mundane moments into a personal time out, and bounce back, feeling good and doing fine.

A Recipe for Relief

What would be the ingredients for an ideal method of handling everyday tensions? Obviously it would have to be quick. After encountering a frustration, busy people frequently have *three minutes or less of available recovery time* before confronting their next responsibility. So a method for resolving problems on the go should contain no more than three or four simple steps.

The perfect technique would be free of negative side effects. It wouldn't lower our level of energy or interfere with motivation. It would enable us to feel both relaxed and alert, at the same time.

You will find thirty techniques in this book that can ease frustrations in three minutes or less. No one is likely to need all thirty, but it's still important to become familiar with them. A method that seems irrelevant today may be perfect for some high-pressure predicament week after next.

Most of these thirty methods could be described as ways of *letting go*. They enable us to release our tensions quickly, and move ahead into positive action. So in this book, to "let go" means to resolve an emotional upset, rapidly and directly.

Many of us assume that it's hard to release upsets. Your mind may tell you that you can't possibly cope with tensions any faster than you do already. Watch as it tries to convince you to hang on to regrets about the past and anxieties over the future. Then try out some methods for letting go, and see what happens.

Recognizing Your Own Progress

When learning something new, it's important to give yourself credit for successes. Be sure to notice whenever you feel a decrease in frustration, stress, or physical tension. At first these changes may be subtle, so watch for the small improvements that let you know you're on the right track.

You'll spot these improvements more easily by developing a sort of *emotional barometer*—an internal signal that tells you when you're starting to feel unhappy. The most reliable barometer is often a particular muscle that gets tight if you're under stress. Does the tension first appear in your face, neck, shoulders, back, chest, or abdomen? Other early warning signs would include an increase in anxiety, a sense of pressure, or noticing that you're holding your breath.

You'll get lots of practice looking for these clues as you learn the methods of *Feel Better Now*. When you run into an upsetting situation, check your emotional barometer, do something to ease the pressure, and then check again to see if you released some tension.

This process itself is a way of letting go. It takes your mind off what's bothering you, while you focus your attention within. And after you've calmed down, you may suddenly see how to solve the original problem.

How to Let Go

Although you'll be learning thirty different ways of reducing tension, most of these methods fall into three simple categories. They're either relaxers, distracters, or releasers.

Relaxers work by easing physical tension. We almost always feel better after our muscles loosen up. Relaxing techniques involve these three steps:

1. Set aside any problems you're worrying about.
2. Use a relaxation technique from this book for two or three minutes.
3. Return to your activities, having taken the edge off the tension you were feeling before.

Distracters follow a similar pattern:

1. Set aside your problems.
2. Focus your attention on something completely different—a brief but total change of pace.

3. Return to your activities with a fresh outlook.

Releasers work in a number of different ways. These techniques have a sort of "triggering" effect that rapidly reduces muscular tension and emotional frustration. People who use these techniques may feel their burdens dropping away, as if a weight had fallen from their shoulders.

Reassuring ourselves with positive ideas is one way to trigger a release. Later in this chapter you'll find a list of reassuring statements that work especially quickly. As another example, reminding yourself of previous successes in coping with tensions may act as a releaser. Remembering that we *can* reduce our upsets increases the odds that we will. We did it before, so we can do it again.

You'll find examples of relaxers, distracters, and releasers in the next few pages. *Feel Better Now* also includes other approaches, such as positive thinking and accelerated problem-solving. Select the ones that work best for you.

If You Are Using Medications

Any good program for coping with emotional upsets may affect one's need for prescribed medications. If you're taking any prescription drug, check with your physician about whether your dosage needs to be adjusted. Some drugs that might be affected include tranquilizers, antidepressants, insulin, muscle relaxants, pain medication, sleeping tablets, and high blood pressure pills.

A Sampler of Strategies

Although you've just begun this book, it isn't too early to experiment with methods for resolving tensions rapidly. And as you continue reading, you will learn many shortcuts, so that you can use these methods with ever-increasing success. You'll find out:

- How to let go of stress in typical real-life situations.
- How to avoid the pitfalls people encounter as they learn to let go.
- How to spot a dozen subconscious reasons why people keep themselves unhappy.

- How to let go of anxiety without sacrificing drive and determination.
- How to remember to use your favorite strategies.

But even here at the beginning of the book, you can benefit by exploring the following techniques:

Method 1: Take a Breather

Usually when we feel upset we begin to hold our breath. To release the breath is one of the most basic forms of letting go.

When you use this technique, put aside any problem that's bothering you. You can come back to it when you want to, but there's no harm in taking a break. Give yourself a three-minute time out in which you breathe slowly, softly, and deeply, closing your eyes if that's appropriate. If you wish, count to five as the air comes in, and to seven as it goes out. (Spending more time on the exhale has a calming, soothing effect.) Imagine your stresses draining away, every time you enjoy that long, leisurely exhalation.

Take a Breather is a relaxation technique, and it also works as a distracter by shifting our thoughts away from problems for a few minutes. The next technique is a "releaser."

Method 2: Simple Affirmations

Repeating a short, positive affirmation can help us cope with emotional tensions. Here are a few examples:

- Right this minute, I can begin to feel better.
- I can be fully relaxed, and fully energized.
- I always have a choice about the way I feel inside
- I can take the edge off tension, whenever I choose.
- Life is too precious to waste on worry.

- I'll do my best, and accept whatever happens.
- Deep down, I know I'll be OK.

Try making up your own examples. Keep them short and keep them positive, avoiding negative words like "not" and "don't." Repetition is important. Repeat your affirmations for a few minutes at least once a day, preferably either out loud or on paper. Try out several affirmations, and see which ones relieve the pressure most rapidly.

Now here's one more tension-releasing technique.

——————□——————

Method 3: Take a Step

When we're upset, it's often because we don't like something that's happening (or that might happen), and we're not sure what to do about it. It helps to ask yourself what *one thing* you can do to start moving in a positive direction. This first step may not solve the problem, but it's hard to solve the problem without taking the first step. Action gives birth to hope, and hope gives birth to further action.

In case you have trouble deciding what to do first, here is a positive action checklist:

- Write down all of your thoughts about the problem.
- List your alternatives, and narrow the choices down to two or three.
- Decide that the situation can't possibly be changed, and begin to adjust to it.
- Tackle the most interesting or enjoyable part of the problem.
- Tackle the easiest part.
- Deal with the most urgent part.
- Seek advice from an expert or an objective friend.

——————□——————

The three methods you've just read about can be combined in the following sequence:

1. Set your problems aside, and breathe softly and deeply for one or two minutes.
2. Every time you take a breath, repeat an affirmation such as, "Right this minute, I can begin to feel better."
3. After calming down, decide whether you want to work on any of your problems. If you do, use the Take a Step technique. Remember to focus on what you *can* do to solve the problem, rather than on what you can't do.

What to expect. At this point you can realistically aim at taking the edge off of minor physical and emotional tensions. You won't get results every time, and sometimes the pressure may even increase because of anxiety about trying new techniques. At first, you may need to use a technique for up to fifteen minutes, but later it may work in seconds.

Try out all kinds of approaches. When you've discovered one or two methods that work especially well, use them repeatedly, *going through the same procedure every time.* Repetition makes the process easier and easier.

As you get better at letting go, your relationships will become more comfortable. You'll find it easier to discipline yourself, so as to control overeating, overspending, and procrastination. You'll develop increased self-esteem. But for now, just enjoy playing with some introductory techniques, and notice which ones work against the minor upsets you'll be using for practice.

The next step is to discover your own most basic tension patterns, and that's the subject of Chapter Two.

Key Ideas from Chapter One

Because life is so complicated, our available recovery time after experiencing frustration is often limited. We need ways of rapidly releasing physical tension and emotional distress—ways of "letting go."

All of us have the ability to let go, using relaxers, distracters, releasers, or a combination of methods. We can cope with problems as they develop, so they don't pile up and become overwhelming. No matter how many challenges we're facing, *we will always have a choice about the way we feel inside.*

The Itch That Can't Be Scratched

Unhappiness comes in dozens of different packages—anger, sadness, anxiety, envy, and guilt, to name a few. All of these varied emotions are triggered by a few basic tension patterns. In this chapter, we'll examine these patterns, and then trace each of them back to *one* underlying cause—a "master mechanism" that generates physical tension and mental distress. Toward the end of the chapter, we'll learn techniques that block this basic tension mechanism.

Let's look at self-frustration syndrome number one.

Pushing

Picture a baboon in the zoo who spots a ripe banana, just a few feet from his cage. He pushes against the bars, forcing and grunting, but the fruit remains inches out of reach.

The baboon used a very basic animal strategy—he *pushed* to reach what he wanted. But brute force didn't do the job. We human beings aren't limited to such simple tactics. We could have reached for the fruit with improvised tools, persuaded people outside the cage to toss us the banana, or even talked ourselves into thinking we weren't hungry in the first place. Yet underneath our rich repertoire of abilities, the old animal instincts persist. Even while pursuing a non-physical goal, we may find ourselves pushing and forcing like the frustrated monkey. We may mentally shove and struggle, revving up our bodies with a brain-fogging surge of adrenalin. Unfortunately, pushing often *prevents* us from getting what we want:

- A salesman is pushing hard to close a deal. The buyer senses his aggressiveness, and backs off.
- Angry at her son's low grades, a mother demands that

he finish his history lesson. He resentfully complies, but the next day he "forgets" to bring his textbook home.

- An accountant can't recall where he filed an important document. The more he tries to remember, the more helpless he feels.

In each of these cases, a person (1) wants to reach a goal, (2) tensely grabs for it, and (3) winds up pushing the goal out of reach.

Look at the ways we create and maintain the attitude of pushing. By hurrying in the morning, some of us start pushing before we even get out the door. Then we negotiate the ordeal of traffic, balancing the contradictory values of speed and survival. At work many of us scurry through a labyrinth of goals and subgoals, and then jump back on the freeway.

Other needs beckon us at home. We try to crowd in our house-cleaning, appliance repairs, eating, reading, shopping, socializing, television, religion, child care, recreation, exercise, humanitarian concerns, and...relaxation. Even in idle moments, the mind is busy wishing and pushing and worrying about the phone call we forgot to make and the raise we're afraid we won't be getting.

Pushing is a painful way to live. Many of us are unaware of the pain; we've endured it so long that it feels normal. But both physically and emotionally, constant forcing and pushing *hurts*.

Bracing: Life in the Dentist's Chair

People push when they want to get something positive. They brace if they want to avoid something negative.

To understand how bracing feels, think about a trip to the dentist. Leaning back in the chair, mouth wedged open, a person's back and legs may start to tighten. The whole body tries to arch upward, as if to shove the discomfort away. With modern dental techniques, these high-stress reactions cause far more anguish than the dental work itself.

Unfortunately, some of us live our entire lives as if we're about to have a molar drilled. Many people are anxious a large percentage of the time, as if their world were about to collapse like a playhouse in a hurricane.

"I walk around braced against a blow, like someone's about to let me have it."

"When I make a mistake I sometimes feel like my father's going to yell at me, even though he hasn't actually done that in years."

Constant bracing keeps people from feeling at peace. They stay on guard, tensing their muscles and holding their breath without knowing it. (Check your own breathing, for example.)

We sometimes brace when we are:

- With someone who's aggravating.
- Tensing up against physical pain.
- Feeling shy in a social setting.
- In a place that is noisy, crowded, or unattractive.

As we practice letting go, we discover that we aren't in the dentist's chair, after all, and most of our on-guard attitudes can be tossed aside like a topcoat in summertime.

Dithering

We frustrate ourselves by struggling for something positive (pushing), or resisting something negative (bracing). Another syndrome might be called dithering. One client provided the following "recipe" for a well-developed dither.

Combine ten pounds of pushing with ten pounds of bracing. Spread both attitudes over 88 problems, and mix at high speed.

It's the combination of multiple problems and hurrying to resolve them right this second that works us into a frenzy. Many of us are addicted to hurrying. Instead of walking, we scurry. We eat as if we've declared war on the entree. Our phone calls are terse, our voices hard-edged. Dithering makes us high strung and off balance. As a harried young mother told me, "I feel like somebody dropped my nervous system into a blender."

People tend to dither:

- While worrying.
- While cramming for an exam or finishing an overdue project.
- When performing multiple tasks, or one task with constant interruptions (tending small children, for example).

It doesn't usually cost any time to refrain from forcing the pace.

We can walk faster with a free-swinging stride than with a neurotic/robotic skitter. At best, hurrying saves us a few seconds while spoiling a great many days.

The *Undivided Awareness* technique is a specific antidote to dithering.

Method 4: Undivided Awareness

Special benefits: Undivided awareness works through "positive distraction," pulling us away from our jumbled, fragmented thoughts. It's an excellent technique to use at work or while carrying out chores at home.

> When you're feeling scattered and confused, look at your watch and commit yourself to focusing complete attention on what you're doing for ten minutes. Don't allow your mind to waver or wander. Let yourself become absorbed in the activity, whether it be straightening the house, talking with your children, or tuning up the car. Maintain a steady, non-frantic pace. After focusing on one thing for ten minutes you're likely to feel calmer, and with practice you can get results in two or three minutes.

There are many patterns of tension, but pushing, bracing, and dithering seem to be the most basic. Our minds push, like a billy goat butting a fence. They brace, like a boxer blocking a punch. They dither, like a cat that got squirted by the garden hose. Our minds react in the same way that animals behave, as they deal with hazards and obstacles. In many ways, the mind behaves as if it were actually a body.

Straining

Pushing, bracing, and dithering all involve a particularly destructive form of tension. It's not the energizing tension a person feels while playing Ping-Pong. It's not the centered concentration that keeps a Zen student sitting bolt upright for three hours of meditation. The pattern we're talking about consists of

> ## tensely wanting or trying
> ## to make a situation turn out "right."

This attitude is the master mechanism in the human mind that generates frustration and physical stress. It is the *number one cause* of destructive emotions, at least among healthy, well-fed individuals who aren't currently threatened with bodily harm.

It's natural to want things to turn out right, but this healthy desire to improve our lives becomes contaminated with exaggerated urgency and compulsiveness. It becomes a forcing, shoving, do-or-die attitude.

> Benson is sitting at a stoplight that's been stuck for five minutes. He begins tensely wanting the signal to go green. The muscles bunch up along his spine, and he holds his breath. Horns are honking now, but he doesn't like to break the law. He thinks of turning right, but that would put him against the traffic on a one-way street. His heart pounds, his body prepares itself for extraordinary feats, and he cannot think at all. An intelligent, competent human being is filled with useless anxiety that goes nowhere and accomplishes nothing.

Benson's only reasonable options were to push down the accelerator and go through or to hold the brake and let other cars go around. But Benson's mind acted as though all the emotional rigmarole would add something useful. That's the mental mistake many of us make dozens of times a day.

"Tensely trying" is an irritating state of mind. We want to soothe it, just as we would want to scratch an itchy mosquito bite. The most obvious way to ease the tension is to solve whatever difficulty is bothering us. Unfortunately, many of us get caught in the following cycle:

- We notice a problem.
- We tense up.
- We fix the problem.
- We notice another problem.
- We tense up.
- We fix the new problem.
- We notice another. (And so on, hour after hour.)

"Tensely trying" becomes an itch that cannot be scratched.

In this book we'll use the words "straining" and "struggling" as shorthand terms for the attitude of tensely trying to make a situation turn out right. These words imply pressure, frustration, weariness, and even physical harm, as when stress leads to an ulcer. They suggest effort without satisfying results.

Here is a list of situations that would trigger straining and struggling in most people. Think about how you would feel in these predicaments.

1. You walk into a restaurant, ravenous, and are told there will be a five-minute wait. After fifteen minutes your mind begins straining for your name to be called. How do you feel, physically and emotionally? When the hostess walks over, do you take a breath and hold it in, exhaling in disappointment when she calls another party?

2. While bowling, you see your ball wobbling down the lane toward the gutter. Do you gesture toward the ball, as if to change its direction through "body English?"

3. What about the times when you can't think of a word that's on the tip of your tongue? Does the mind struggle to make the word appear? Does this resemble the way it struggles to put the ball back on course or get the hostess to call your name?

4. You're riding in a car, and the driver is careless. Do you silently struggle for control? When a truck swerves in front of you, does your foot push down as if you were hitting the brakes? Do you have impulses to turn the steering wheel?

If these situations would bother you, see if you can recall the sense of straining—tensely trying to make things turn out right. Start noticing when that feeling begins to creep up on you. Spot it quickly whenever you can. That feeling of strain is the enemy.

Pictures, Words, and Relaxing Sounds

The habit of inwardly straining and struggling creates an unhealthy psychological climate. No matter what's happening on the outside, we feel under pressure internally. We need ways of quickly improving the "weather" inside of our minds. Certain words and mental images can do this, and the right combination of sounds can also help us calm down rapidly. First of all, here's how your imagination can create a special stress-free zone in your own mind:

Method 5: The Sanctuary

Special benefits: Provides an instant change of scene, a mental mini-vacation from everyday concerns.

> If you could have a safe, comfortable place to go whenever you wanted to, what would it be? It doesn't have to be a real place or even a place that could exist. Would it be a cabin in the mountains? A forest glen that no one else knows how to find? A private spaceship? A garden in Tahiti? A secret castle? Write down or describe to yourself what this safe, comfortable place would be like.

When you're going to sleep at night, imagine visiting this special sanctuary. You might see yourself resting there, listening to music, or visiting with a friend. After you've done this several times, you can use the same fantasy during the day. Close your eyes or look down for a few minutes, and enter your personal retreat.

Now here's a relaxation technique you can use when pushing and bracing leads to muscular tension:

----□----

Method 6: Think Soft

Special benefits: Enables us to relax a very specific part of the body, as if we were directing a healing beam of energy at a sore shoulder or a stiff neck.

> Locate a tight muscle somewhere in your body. Imagine that the tension is turning into something soft, like candle wax that's getting warmer and warmer and finally melting away. Feel the candle wax drip, and enjoy the way your muscles begin to relax. Some people imagine the tension turning into clay, cotton, foam rubber, or Jell-O, or they simply think, "Softer, softer."

----□----

If thinking soft eases the pressure by twenty percent or more, this method is a good one for you to practice. Eventually you should get results in just sixty seconds while sitting at your desk, doing the dishes, or waiting in line at a fast-food restaurant.

Use any picture that helps you let go, drawing upon whatever you associate with peace and confidence. Try using animals, for instance. Because cats are such unruffled creatures, you might visualize yourself with the face of a sleeping kitten. Or perhaps you'd enjoy the powerful softness of a purring lion or lioness. To relax your face, you might think of it as a magnificent flower in full bloom. Picture its rich colors and the crisp green of the leaves. It's smooth, fresh, and healthy, and you can sense a cool breeze flowing over the petals. Allow yourself to take a deep leisurely breath, as you feel the tension lines dissolving.

You can also use images that suggest an instant release of tension. Imagine your distress as a tight rubber band, and suddenly let go of one end. Picture a problem as if it were a fishing line that's hooked on an old inner tube, and then cut the line so the problem drifts away. Pretend you're holding your troubles in your hand. Slowly open the hand and let the troubles fall to earth or float up to the sky.

In addition to images, certain words and phrases can help dissolve tension. Words have an almost magical impact upon us. Much of what makes us happy or sad is our reaction to messages such as, "You made an 'A,' " or "I love you."

----------------◻----------------

Method 7: Word Magic

Special benefits: Breaks the automatic flow of thoughts with a lulling word or phrase.

> Choose a simple word, such as "peace," "rest," "quiet," "relax," "calm," or "tranquility." You can also count, "1001," "1002," etc., or use phrases such as, "deeper and deeper relaxation." Repeat the word or phrase silently for sixty seconds or longer. Breathe slowly and deeply. If possible, close your eyes or look down. As various thoughts pass through your mind, let them remain in the background while you focus on the soothing word or phrase. (Do not use this process while driving.)

----------------◻----------------

The first few times, practice Word Magic in a quiet place for at least ten minutes, so that your mind will learn to associate the technique with relaxation. Eventually it will work in just two or three minutes.

The Sanctuary, Think Soft, and Word Magic all involve *positive changes in what you see and hear.* Think about your own visual and auditory environment. How could you nourish your mind with relaxing pictures and sounds? Simply purchasing an attractive calendar for your home or office can make a noticeable difference. And of course, music is one of the quickest and most effective mood-changers available. Three kinds of recordings are especially useful:

- Music that is consistently slow and quiet. It should be bright, rather than melancholy. Solo flute, harp, or piano are often good choices.

- Fast, lively, energetic music.
- Any recording that helps *you* feel happy and comfortable.

Find something that fits one or more of these categories and keep it handy—preferably where you can see it every day. You may want to have one recording at home, a cassette tape to play in the car (even on a portable tape recorder), and another for work, if that's appropriate.

———————□———————

Method 8: The Gift of Music

Special benefits: Music engages the right side of the brain, and pulls us away from the anxious, repetitive thought patterns of the left hemisphere.

> When you're under pressure, tell yourself that you deserve a change of pace. Take a few minutes to fill your mind with music. Then keep the music playing quietly in the background as you continue your daily activities. (Humming or whistling or even letting a song repeat itself in your mind can also be effective.)

———————□———————

In Chapter Three we'll continue to learn step-by-step methods for letting go. Learning these methods is like learning a new game. You'll be playing with your moods and attitudes, to see what makes them shift. It's an absorbing, satisfying game, and the payoffs will last for a lifetime.

Key Ideas from Chapter Two

In this chapter we've looked at the opposite of letting go, the patterns of pushing, bracing, and dithering. Underlying all of these is the attitude of straining—tensely wanting or trying to make a situation turn out right. Straining triggers anxiety, stress, and conflict. If we let go of struggling, such upsets will deflate like a bunch of leaky balloons. One way to let go is to change the internal "climate" of the mind through relaxing words, images, and sounds.

Begin with the Body

When my clients first experimented with letting go, they seesawed back and forth between excitement and bewilderment. We were working with the kinds of problems described in Chapters One and Two— time pressures, muscular tensions, personality conflicts, and other everyday annoyances. They could relieve these upsets more rapidly than they had ever imagined. It was like discovering a passbook to a savings account that they had somehow forgotten existed.

But it was also like grasping at quicksilver, or trying to nail jelly to the wall. Letting go seemed unpredictable. A person would neatly dissolve an emotional upset, and the next week hold on to the same upset as if it were the crown jewels. Some could release anger, but not sadness, while for others it was the reverse. Letting go was as elusive as smoke, a friendly will-o'-the-wisp that played hide and seek with our minds.

Eventually we learned to pin down this slippery phenomenon. We found that letting go occurs most quickly and consistently when people use a three-step sequence of *tuning in, preparing,* and *releasing.* You don't need to go through these three steps every time you let go, but it's a good idea to do so when you're dealing with especially difficult problems.

Let's consider an example of this three-stage process. Imagine we can eavesdrop on the thoughts of David, both before and after he learns techniques for feeling better rapidly. David has been in sales work for fifteen years. His two boys are in junior high. In watching them grow up, David has decided he likes kids enough to go into school teaching.

Sitting at the office, David thinks:

I'm awfully reluctant to quit my sales job. I used to love it, but it's gotten stale. Teaching sounds great, but what if I'm no good at it? I'll feel like I crawled out on limb and someone sawed it off.

Here I am thirty-five years old, feeling awkward as a teenager again. (David's stomach is getting tighter and he's developing a headache. He fidgets in his chair and looks at his watch.) It's almost lunch time. I think I'll go have a gin and tonic.

I swear, I've got so much junk stuffed into my head, it feels like a trash compactor. (He smiles ruefully, lightens up for a minute, and then sinks back into depression.)

Maybe I'll just stick to sales and forget about becoming Teacher of the Year. (He knocks off early and goes to lunch.)

After learning to let go of tensions, David's thoughts have changed:

(Tuning-in phase) I'm reluctant to quit my job. I'd better tune into the tension I feel about that. I'm anxious, and my stomach is jumpy, so my "emotional barometer" says I'm pretty upset. How am I scaring myself? (Pause.) I'm wanting to be certain I'll be a good teacher, but there's no way to be sure until I try it out.

I need to let go of fretting about the future. (To begin *preparing to let go,* David asks himself whether tensing up his abdomen will help him decide what to do. This usually amuses him, so it's a good way of preparing to let go. Then he moves on to the *releasing phase,* and imagines his mind becoming still, like a clear pool of water. He has used the still-water picture about twenty times, and it's starting to work very easily.) I think I was getting a headache, but it's easing up now. I've reduced my discomfort by about fifty percent. (He sits quietly, repeating the technique for another two minutes.) Now—what can I do that's useful? I could check into the schooling I'll need to become a teacher. (He picks up the phone.)

Here we have a cutaway view of the same person's thought processes on two different occasions. The second column shows David *tuning in* to his own emotional barometer (physical sensations in his abdomen), *preparing* to let go by asking whether the tension is necessary, and then *releasing* the pressure by using a relaxing image.

Let's continue to explore the connection between muscle tension and emotional tension.

An Experiment in Angry Relaxation

A few years ago I went to a religious service, in a most irreligious frame of mind. A friend had let me down, and I was livid with anger. It was one of those gigantic trivialities that matter so much until the next tempest in a teapot comes along. As I sat down I felt justified and even pleased at being irritated. I had a right to be mad!

In time, that self-righteous glow of indignation became tarnished by the increasingly obvious pain in my neck, back, and chest. I liked being angry, except that it was starting to hurt.

Suddenly I had a novel idea. Since anger felt good and tension felt bad, I could keep feeling angry while at the same time relaxing my body. So I carefully went through my muscles, releasing tightness in my toes, feet, ankles, and so on. I nearly laughed out loud as I finished. At the moment I relaxed the last part of my body (my face and head), the anger vanished completely. It seemed silly that I'd wanted to hold on to that feeling just twenty minutes before.

For many individuals unhappiness is primarily the ache and pinch of tense muscles. They are *holding on to unhappiness* by keeping their muscles in a chronic state of contraction. When they relax, a lot of the unhappiness melts away, even though the original cause of the upset hasn't changed. The tension is frequently worse than the problem itself. Our problems may bruise us, but the frustration we feel about having problems is what can crush us.

Quick Relief for Tense Muscles

To untorque a stiff neck or a tight stomach, use the technique from Chapter One called Take a Breather, or one of the five methods listed in this chapter. Don't forget—*Feel Better Now* includes thirty techniques because *no single technique fits every person and every problem.* As you read, look for the strategies that appeal to you the most.

Hold the other methods in reserve, but concentrate on methods that fit your personality and your life situation.

---□---

Method 9: Twelve-Point Tension Release

Special benefits: No other technique targets every one of the major accumulation points for physical tension.

> A few times each day, go through the following sequence. (In all cases, respect any physical limitations you may have.) Gently roll your *eyes* in a circle twice in one direction, and then twice the opposite way. Look at something in the distance, and then focus on something nearby. Frown and tense the eye muscles a bit, and release. Go down to the *jaw,* and yawn a couple of times. Loosen the *neck* by nodding, then slowly turning your head from side to side. Bring your *shoulders* up to your ears and down again. To free up your *wrists,* roll your hands in circles. Make fists and unclench them to relax the *hands.* Returning to the *torso,* take three very deep breaths. Then gently arch your *spine* forward and backward, and side to side. Tighten and relax your *buttocks,* and then your *calves.* Roll your feet in circles to loosen the *ankles.* Then conclude by curling your toes under so that your *feet* arch upward, three times. (If it would be inappropriate to actually move your body, you can gain most of the benefit by moderately tightening and relaxing each area.)

---□---

You've just dissolved about fifty percent of the tightness in twelve major tension points. You've also distracted yourself from whatever was bothering you, so you've reaped a double benefit.

———————☐———————

Method 10: Seven-Eleven Breathing

Special benefits: This is a good technique for reducing extreme physical tension, without needing to leave the stressful situation.

> Breathe very slowly and completely, so that each cycle takes about twenty seconds. You should feel some stretching as you do this, but don't strain. Count to seven on the inhale, eleven on the exhale.

———————☐———————

It will take concentration to stretch out the breath that much, and many people find the process quite absorbing. "By slowing down my breath, this technique helps me withdraw into myself for a few minutes," wrote a secretarial student, "and there's something soothing about that long, long exhale."

The very full inhale stretches the ribs gently, softening the tensions that develop in the intercostal muscles. The exaggerated exhale relaxes the abdomen. If you feel lightheaded when you first try Seven-Eleven Breathing, do it for a shorter period and breathe less deeply.

A salesman tried this at a meeting of his company's reps. "It was actually hard to inhale and exhale fully, because I was sitting there holding my breath very tightly. I had no idea I was doing that. After a few minutes I noticed my face and neck relaxing."

———————□———————

Method 11: Move!

Special benefits: Some people dissolve tension more easily through movement than through any other avenue.

Express your feelings physically, by exercising, dancing, or acting out what you're feeling (e.g. shadowboxing when you're angry). Even a brief spurt of activity will energize you and alter your mood. Walking rapidly while breathing forcefully is effective, and so is doing a few deep knee bends. Of course, take care not to overextend your own capabilities.

———————□———————

Method 12: Self-Massage

Special benefits: Highly dependable relief for stiff muscles.

Even during a busy day, there are dozens of potential "mini-vacations" when you can take two or three minutes to relax. During some of those breaks you can unobtrusively rub one of your physical stress points. Rub gently, and close your eyes if you can. Some places that are easy to reach include:

- The "frown spot." Rub softly in slow circles where your eyebrows join, just above the nose.
- Back of the neck. Squeeze gently with one hand.
- The jaw. There's an important muscle just behind the place where your back teeth come together. Rub there

and see if it feels tender.
- Tops of the shoulders. Knead these muscles with the thumb and fingers of one hand.
- Soles of the feet. If you're on a shopping expedition, sit in the car and rub your sore feet before trudging into the next store.

-------------◻-------------

A more discreet version of this method involves resting your hand on a tight muscle and imagining heat from the hand penetrating deeply into the tense area. A livelier approach is to lightly slap yourself from head to toe. It's both relaxing and energizing.

Body Release

Body Release is a more fully developed version of some techniques we've considered earlier, such as "thinking soft."

-------------◻-------------

Method 13: Body Release

Special benefits: A very thorough technique, because it follows the three steps described at the beginning of this chapter—tuning in, preparing, and releasing. In addition, by using this method people learn to spot stress before it builds up.

When your body feels tight from stress or emotional upset:

1. Locate a tense group of muscles and experience them, without necessarily trying to relax them.
2. Take a moment to feel how much energy you're expending to keep these muscles tight.
3. Imagine them becoming soft and pliable, as if they were turning into clay or warm candle wax.

-------------◻-------------

Let's consider the three steps, one by one.

1. Locate a tense group of muscles and experience them, without necessarily trying to relax them. (Tuning-in phase)

In this step you zero in on the place where you're hurting yourself the worst, the center of the whole system of muscles under pressure.

To *experience* a tension means to feel it just as it is, in a real and vivid way. That's not the same as thinking about it, talking about it, imagining it, remembering it, worrying over it, or vaguely noticing it. Experiencing muscular tension means you know how it feels this very minute: "Yes, that's the way my shoulders are scrunching up right now." Perhaps the muscles are pushing, as when the neck juts forward impatiently, or bracing, like an arm that's about to receive a hypodermic injection. When you sense exactly how your body is tensing itself, it may automatically relax.

Try out step one for yourself. Find a spot in your body that's tight, and turn your own "mental searchlight" on the place that pinches the most. As you hold your attention there, the pain may soften, so it isn't as pointed any more.

2. Take a moment to feel how much energy you're expending to keep these muscles tight. (Preparing phase)

Those muscles are working hard. Think about the constant flow of energy that holds the body taut for hours or even days. The muscles are activated, but they aren't going anywhere. It's like automobile tires spinning in the mud, using up gas without moving forward. It's so tiring, and so unnecessary.

Step two helps us remember that being unhappy is hard work. It literally takes more effort to frown than to smile. We are so accustomed to kinking up our bodies in distorted positions that we think it's the easiest way to be. It may be the most automatic way, but it's not the easiest.

3. Imagine the muscles becoming soft and pliable, as if they were turning into clay or warm candle wax. (Releasing phase)

As indicated in Chapter Two, you can imagine your muscles turning into a variety of soft substances—cotton, clouds, Jell-O, foam rubber, heated butter, or clear, soothing water. Step three could also consist of:

- Imagining that a liquid or a soft breeze is flowing through the tense area.

- Tightening the muscle and then relaxing it.
- Pretending the muscle is already relaxed, which will often trigger real relaxation.

As always, we allow letting go to happen, without forcing it. We needn't strain to get rid of straining.

One student used Body Release to diminish the fear of his supervisor. He suspected that his supervisor intimidated him because of a resemblance to his grandfather.

> **Carlos:** Both of them have a weathered face, and big dark eyes that get shiny black if you do something wrong. In my dreams I could see those eyes, and I'd wake up frightened. I feel pressure in my stomach just talking about the Old Man.

> **Chris:** Your stomach seems to be a good barometer of your tension level. *Experience the tension in your stomach, and describe it.*

> **Carlos:** It's a dull, pulsing ache, around my navel. It's sort of pushing, but it mainly feels braced. I'll bet I used to brace myself around Grandpa, because I was afraid he might hit me.

> **Chris:** Go into the pinpoint spot in the middle of that braced feeling. *Feel how much energy you're expending.*

> **Carlos:** A lot, definitely. (He feels it for about half a minute.) Now there's less pain.

> **Chris:** That's typical. When we notice how we're holding our bodies off-kilter, we start shifting back into balance. So you experienced the tight spot, and you saw how tiring it is to keep it tense. Let's go to step three. *Imagine those muscles softening.* It's all right to stop bracing. You're here today, safe and secure.

> **Carlos:** It's as if I'd forgotten it was OK to be comfortable. The pain is down to about ten percent of what it was when I started.

> **Chris:** If the pain in your stomach persists, do go to a doctor. But if it's emotional tension, Body Release should make a big difference. I'd also suggest Seven-Eleven Breathing to relax the tightness in your abdomen.

Here's another example: Glen and his family are being visited by a couple from out of town. After the first day of the visit, Glen thinks:

> I like Kathy, but Bruce is driving me batty. He's such a know-it-all, with his sneering little jibes. Let's see what my body starts feeling when I picture Bruce. I'm keeping my shoulders rigid. No need to lock them into place. The pressure is mostly in my right shoulder. It doesn't need to work so hard . . . good, good. (Glen spends five minutes with the Body Release technique.) I feel stronger. I'm actually becoming excited about getting this off my chest.

During the conversation with Bruce, Glen refrained from knotting his stomach or freezing up his shoulders. Some of his fear and anger returned, but not as badly. Glen projected confidence, and Bruce agreed to sheath his verbal stiletto.

Notice that Glen took effective action to eliminate what was aggravating him. He didn't say, "Since I'm so good at letting go, I'll just let Bruce keep slicing away!" This story also shows the value of *fantasy practice.* If we fantasize a situation beforehand, and let go of the tension, we'll be calmer when we face the actual situation.

It's valuable to actually experiment with Body Release, because most of us learn better by personal experimentation than by merely reading words. Even if you're not planning to use this technique, try it out as an exercise. Go through these three steps, slowly and consciously.

1. Locate and experience a tense group of muscles, without necessarily trying to relax them.
2. Notice how much energy you're expending to keep these muscles tight.
3. Imagine them becoming soft and pliable, as if they were turning into clay or warm candle wax.

As you practice, remember that the mind may resist these techniques, dwelling upon your so-called failures rather than recognizing your insights and breakthroughs. Don't worry. Just try out various suggestions, and notice which ones feel best.

Physical relaxation takes the sting out of most emotional upsets. But it's even better to combine a relaxed body with a healthy, positive outlook. Chapter Four will show how we can shift our own attitudes, quickly and directly.

Key Ideas from Chapter Three

For many of us, what we call "unhappiness" is mostly the aching tightness of our muscles when we're under stress. Some of the most effective techniques for quickly coping with stresses involve three specific phases—tuning in to the tension, preparing to relax, and letting go. Body Release is a good example of such a technique, and we'll learn others later on.

From Demands to Preferences

I once had a client who referred to himself as the Great Dictator. His acquaintances would never have described Andy's behavior as dictatorial. They saw him as a head-nodding people pleaser, too agreeable for his own good. But in the kingdom of his own thoughts, Andy was a tyrant, imperiously judging how everything ought to be. Secretly, silently, he criticized his friends, relatives, co-workers, and even household appliances.

The Great Dictator began to learn flexibility after being introduced to the work of Ken Keyes (last name rhymes with eyes). What follows are some ideas that build upon Ken's concept of "demands versus preferences." To find out what he himself says, you can read his best known work, *Handbook to Higher Consciousness*, or his more recent volume, *Gathering Power Through Insight and Love*.

In talking to Andy about demands and preferences, I suggested that there are two different ways of responding to a problem.

1. "I cannot be happy unless this problem is solved." (I link my happiness to the outcome.)
2. "If the problem isn't solved, I can still feel okay." (I disconnect my happiness from the outcome.)

The first attitude could be called "demanding." We are telling ourselves we *must* have what we want. There's no flexibility; we're locked into our own rigid expectations. The second attitude is more like "preferring." We prefer to have things our way, but we can accept an alternative result.

An important clarification. In this book, the terms "demands" and "preferences" are given a special meaning. They have to do with whether a person is *linking happiness* to the way a situation comes out. So we're not talking about demanding words or actions, but rather a demanding attitude.

A woman whose purse is being wrestled away by a robber may appropriately demand that the robber return the purse. She may also demand that the police pursue the thief. But later on if she believes she cannot be happy without the purse, she is doing herself a disservice. That is the sort of inner, mental demand that ends up frustrating us.

To return to the Great Dictator, Andy immediately realized that the idea of demands versus preferences could help him. As he put it, "To crawl through life chaining my own happiness to whether or not I get my way is a prescription for misery. At any given moment, I'll either feel unhappy because something is wrong, or happy but insecure because something might *start* going wrong. I don't think happiness plus constant insecurity is really happiness, any more than good health plus a terrible cold is the same as 'being well.'

"When I demand a certain outcome, I immediately throw away my sense of proportion. Every victory or defeat becomes a Big Deal, even though I'll have forgotten it by next Thursday. Next Thursday I'll probably be coping with a new set of big deals."

In transforming demands into preferences, Andy used the idea of surfing, based on watching his teenage son ride the waves. Andy first practiced surfing on little "waves"—his reactions to a rainy day, a rattle in the car, a moldy loaf of bread, or a phone call at two a.m. (wrong number). Then he worked up to more difficult issues. So in time, the Great Dictator became the Great Surfer.

Eventually it's possible for people to disconnect their happiness from very serious problems. Ken Keyes, for instance, needs to use a wheelchair. I suppose he would prefer to be able to stand, walk, and run. But is he supposed to be miserable forever as a result? That's what would happen if his preference were also a demand.

Letting go is not a rationalization: "It makes no difference whether I can walk." Letting go is based on the truth: "It is realistically possible to be a happy human being and use a wheelchair to get around."

Preferential thinking is a key to coping with illness and chronic physical pain. Obviously medical help is important, but sometimes the pain of arthritis or other long-term conditions will persist in spite of pills and operations. Pushing and bracing against the pain only makes it worse. We can learn to tolerate chronic discomfort while we focus on what's positive in our lives. Some people use affirmations such as: "I can enjoy myself every day, even if my body is uncomfortable." "Physical discomfort is only a small part of my life," or "I allow the feeling in my neck to remain in the background."

It's important to recognize that when we change demands into preferences we are not lowering our standards or giving up our goals. Calling something a preference does not imply that it's trivial; greater flexibility is a step forward, not a matter of settling for less. We still want whatever we want, and we still strive to get it. And if we don't get it, our day (week) (month) (life) isn't ruined.

Unmasking Pseudo-Problems

How far can we carry the idea of changing demands to preferences? Is it possible that most of our frustrations are not even problems at all? What's the difference between a problem that's real and one that is a non-problem, a pseudo-problem?

We can consider a frustration to be a pseudo-problem if:

- It does us no physical harm.
- It does not prevent happiness in people who have a basically positive outlook.

A real problem (1) harms us physically or (2) triggers unhappiness even if we approach it with a constructive attitude. But a pseudo-problem leads to unhappiness only for people who cooperate with the hassle and let it get them down.

The tenser we become, the more we create pseudo-problems, and this is true for two reasons. First, tension itself feels unpleasant and this adds an unnecessary layer of discomfort. Second, when we're tense, we're more likely to add *surplus meaning* to an already negative situation. Surplus meaning makes a problem seem worse than it is.

Here's an example: Raymond hands his boss a report, and the boss says it's all wrong. He'll need to work an hour late revising what he's done. Does staying late hurt Raymond physically? No. Would it trigger an upset even in a person with a positive, constructive attitude? Moderately. So he has a real, but moderate problem.

Raymond can easily make the situation seem worse than it is. If he becomes physically tense, he's got not only an hour's inconvenience, but also a headache or a pain in his abdomen. Furthermore, he can pile on surplus meanings such as: "I always get a raw deal," or "The boss has it in for me." He ends up with several unnecessary stresses, on top of a simple one-hour inconvenience.

Expectations

Unreasonable demands often grow out of unrealistic expectations. When we assume that life should be heaven, it begins to resemble hell. Many of us unconsciously demand that:

- People always like us.
- People always treat us fairly.
- People know our needs without our telling them.
- We are never bothered by painful emotions.
- We are not getting any older.
- We are always making progress, without backsliding.
- We are never unexpectedly inconvenienced.
- If we take a risk, it inevitably pays off.
- Someone or something will finally come along and make life turn out perfectly.

Do any of these demands sound familiar? We human beings want lots of guarantees, which only guarantees lots of frustration. "Disappointment is the caboose on the train of expectation."

From Demands to Preferences

Here's a way to free yourself from rigid expectations.

---□---

Method 14: Changing Demands into Preferences

Special benefits: This technique is an ideal antidote to rigidity and perfectionism.

When you're feeling dissatisfied, identify the demand at the core of the unhappy feeling. It will help if you ask yourself, "What do I think I *must* have in order to be happier?" Realize that it's fine to *prefer* whatever you like, but that *demanding* it may be making you tense. Allow the demand to soften into a preference, and then do whatever you can to fulfill your preference.

---□---

Notice that this strategy contains an anti-copout clause: "Do whatever you can to fulfill your preference." In this way, you are consciously reprogramming your mind, *combining relaxation with positive action* rather than with helpless passivity.

How to do it. One key to making this method work is to identify what you're demanding. It helps if you say something like, "I'm assuming I have to be angry because I got catsup on my slacks," "I'm linking my happiness to whether the snow stops falling," or "I'm refusing to feel good because my budget doesn't balance."

We typically imagine we can't feel good until:

- We have plenty of money.
- The work day is over.
- They turn off that jackhammer next door.
- Our stiff neck relaxes.
- Our spouse or our child shapes up.
- We know how our relationship will turn out.
- We can stop hurrying for a while.
- The traffic light changes.
- Someone tells us we're doing OK.
- We lose thirty pounds.
- It's lunchtime.

It's easier to turn these demands into preferences if we view them from a larger perspective. The mind tends to zoom in on every problem as if we were looking at it under a magnifying glass, blowing up small annoyances into large aggravations. We need to compensate for the magnifying glass effect, by stepping back and seeing our problems from a distance. This widens the "picture frame," and cuts little hassles down to size. Here are *five ways to put problems in perspective:*

1. Remember that whatever you're dealing with today is a lot like other challenges you've handled all your life. You'll either solve it, work hard and overcome it, maneuver around it, endure it till it goes away, learn to manage it, learn to accept it, or realize that it's actually not a problem. You've found ways of coping before, and you'll find ways again. The "new" problem isn't the exotic animal it seems to be. It may look like a dragon, but it's only the same old bull.

2. Ask yourself how many times a negative event is likely to occur in a lifetime. If you've been driving for twenty years and just had a five-hundred-dollar stereo stolen from your car, that means twenty-five dollars per year in auto theft losses. Naturally you wish it hadn't happened, but is twenty-five dollars a year worth an attack of colitis?

3. Remind yourself that whatever you lost will probably be available once again. So your son snitched the last piece of Black Forest Cake. So what? Chocolate *is.*

4. Follow the example of Andy and ask, "Will this issue still bother me a week from now?" Often we upset ourselves about matters that seem insignificant within an hour.

5. Call to mind your own central values, based on your religious beliefs or your personal philosophy. Stand your problems up alongside these core values, and see which is taller. One fellow puts minor irritants in perspective by reminding himself, "All I need is my health and my family. Everything else is gravy."

Here's how one man used the demands versus preferences approach:

> Johnnie called me up and said, "Hey, Casey, do you want to go fishing Saturday?" He's kind of boring, so I told him I was busy. Later I found out that he was mad, and now I feel guilty.
>
> There's a bunch of demands in there, such as, "Only people I like a lot should want to spend time with me." Also, nobody should ever be mad at me. That I really hate. Well, I do wish nobody was ever mad at me, but it's pretty unrealistic to demand something like that.
>
> As I think about it now, I'm kind of settling down. Now comes the part about doing what I can to get what I want— which is to mend my fences with Johnnie. I wouldn't mind spending a little while with him. I just didn't want to go out for a whole day. I'll call him up and we'll have a drink. That's what I should have suggested when he phoned me in the first place.

As another example, think about trying to help someone who never seems to get any better. Suppose a psychotherapist, teacher, religious leader, supervisor, or parent is trying to help a client, student, congregant, employee, or child. The person who's being helped keeps resolving to straighten up—and then lapses back into the same old habits. Before long, the "helper" will feel like committing mayhem. It's important to ask, "Am I still OK even if this person never changes? Can I feel good about myself, even if I can't fix everybody on earth?"

Exploring the technique. One way to practice turning demands into preferences is to think of some time when you made a mistake, and there were negative consequences. Do not pick an incident that is emotionally loaded, but pick something that's a little bit embarrassing.

Reflect on what happened as a result of your error. This will probably "push your buttons," and you'll start feeling twinges of discomfort. Notice precisely what you are demanding—what you believe you have to have in order to feel better. Perhaps you're saying you can't be happy because you made an error, or because someone is upset with you. Realize that linking your happiness to these issues is harmful, and allow the demand to moderate into a preference. It may help if you use the five suggestions listed a few pages ago under the heading "How to do it."

Happiness Blockers

If you don't feel better after attempting to change demands into preferences, be on the alert for a happiness blocker. A happiness blocker is a message from the mind telling you that you cannot...should not...must not...feel good right now. It's as if your mind is occupied by a sales representative for misery, who gets a commission every time it convinces you to be gloomy. The salesperson in your mind sometimes slips you a little happiness blocker, whispering that you ought to feel a tiny bit miffed. And sometimes it shouts hysterically about how anybody in your predicament would feel absolutely horrible.

Consider the case of a man who's driving to a job interview and has a flat tire. As he pulls over to the shoulder, he is happiness-blocking with great gusto.

> I'll be late for the interview, and they won't even see me.
> If they do, I'll be all frustrated because I've had to hurry
> so. I'm such a fool for not checking my tires. Part of my
> jack may be missing, and I'll have to call the tow truck.
> Maybe the tire will be wiped out, and I'll have to get a new
> one. Money! Maybe my spare won't have any air in it, or

maybe it'll blow on the way. After I finish I'll look disgusting, with grease all over my clothes. I'll have to keep job hunting, and I hate it. I'll run out of savings, too...Maybe I unconsciously caused this incident. My therapist says that I sabotage myself...Now that the car is up, maybe it's going to fall off the jack and roll down the street. I must look pretty dumb to the people driving by. Damn! This is hard work. I'm hot and sweaty...Now it's done. If I drive like the devil I'll only be a little bit late, but then I might have an accident. Why do I always have such wretched luck?

Can you see how each of these thoughts tends to sell him on being unhappy? Because he wasn't perfect about maintaining his tires, he was supposed to feel inferior, and therefore unhappy. Because he was sweating, he was supposed to be uncomfortable. (He might have had the same feeling while gardening on a warm day, but that could have been very satisfying. The mind has a complex and inconsistent set of criteria for deciding whether a sensation should feel terrible or terrific.)

It would be strange if this fellow were delighted at his misfortune, but if he thought in terms of preferences the situation would seem tolerable. He would be more likely to notice alternatives, such as calling to say he'd be late. He would do less catastrophizing. Nobody loves a blowout, but it's not the end of the world.

We might imagine that if our life circumstances were comfortable enough, we would stop presenting ourselves with happiness blockers. Unfortunately, the inflation of "needs" prevents this from happening. Need inflation means that once we achieve a certain level of success, affluence, and comfort, we inflate our expectations. We treat these new expectations as a demand instead of as icing on the cake. The mind raises our minimum standards as predictably as the officials at a track meet raise the high jump bar.

---◻︎---

Method 15: Self-Questioning

Special benefits: Neutralizes happiness blockers, by giving us new perspective on pressure situations.

When you suspect you're exaggerating the significance of a problem, ask yourself some of the following questions:

- Is this really a Great Big Deal?
- Is anything truly important at risk right now?
- Is this any worse than what I've handled before?
- Will this seem important in two weeks?
- Is this worth making myself sick over?
- Is this worth dying for?
- And of course, the classic: What's the worst thing likely to happen, and would I be able to cope with that?

---◻︎---

Learning to Spot Your Demands

Spotting a demand as soon as it appears can help you head off tension. Think about various situations in which you tell yourself it's time to be unhappy. In these circumstances, the mind tends to get locked into the problem. For instance, think about how it feels when you cannot find a phone number. Does the mind grab ahold of the task, chomping down on it like a bulldog? Perhaps you start tossing papers to and fro in frustration: "I know it's here somewhere!"

That locked-in, hooked-up attitude, as if the mind cannot rest until it untangles the matter, is the signal that demand has crowded out preference. The preferential part of you has been pushed out into the cold—and it probably knows where you put the phone number. (Memory researchers agree that we recall things much more rapidly when we're relaxed.)

Here are some other frustrating situations. If you think about how you would respond to these problems, that will help you recognize what an inner demand feels like to you.

1. The top flies off the blender, and your walls are decorated with gazpacho.
2. Your daughter leaves the wrapper open on the bread...and the cap off the toothpaste tube.
3. Your husband is glued to a book all the time.
4. Your wife nags you to stop reading so much.
5. It rains unexpectedly, and you look like a cat that went for a swim.
6. Your evening paper is sopping up a mud puddle.

It's certainly human to assume that these situations *have* to improve before we can feel better. That's the attitude of demandingness—a powerful psychological toxin. When we demand less, we wind up receiving more.

To Climb the Mountains, Practice on the Molehills

At this point you know several different methods for letting go of inner strain and struggle. As you practice these methods, remember to start with fairly minor issues. Stay away from intensely emotional subjects for a while. A beginning piano student *can* play notes, but that doesn't mean the first lesson should occur at Carnegie Hall. Instead, the student starts with five-finger exercises. Your life presents you with lots of minor snags and irritations, such as those triggered by a traffic tie-up or a cross remark from a shopkeeper. Every little hassle can become an opportunity, because it gives you a chance to practice. Later, dealing with more serious issues, you will have laid a solid foundation for success.

Here are some molehill-sized problems that will help you get the knack of letting go.

1. Traffic. This is an ideal training ground, because most of us grapple with it daily. (*Caution:* Some people need to devote full attention to their driving in order to be safe. If this is true of you, don't carry out mental exercises behind the wheel.)

Experiment #1: Let go of pushing. As you set out in your car, notice how you respond every time you encounter an obstacle, such as stop signs, stop lights, and slow-moving motorists. Do you lean forward, gripping the steering wheel, as if to force the other cars out of the way? Suggest to yourself that you could "push" a little bit less.

Experiment #2: Let go of bracing. Whenever a threat comes your way—icy conditions, debris on the road, or a police car in your rear view mirror—observe the tension in your reactions. Sometimes the tension may be valuable; a surge of adrenalin may help you negotiate a panic stop, for example. But after you're safe, does your emotional barometer continue to read "storm warning?" Imagine the tension melting away, by thinking of it as warm candle wax or heated butter.

The highway is a good place to use the Undivided Awareness technique. For five miles, focus completely on your driving, and ignore all other thoughts. Notice the movement of cars around you, hear the sound of traffic, and check your rear view mirror. Give yourself permission to simply drive, so that you take a vacation from thinking about twenty things at once. If you block out extraneous thoughts, you may arrive at your destination more relaxed than you were when you started out.

If you travel via public transportation, you can let go of tensions about late buses, subway tokens that don't work, and shady characters eyeing your purse or wallet.

2. Reading. You may not think of what you're doing right now as stressful, yet many of us start holding our breath every time we read a single paragraph. Are your eyes and forehead tense? Perhaps the muscles seem to be pushing, especially if you're reading rapidly. Exaggerate the pushing sensation for a moment, and then let the muscles soften. And what about mental tension? For instance, you may be straining to understand certain ideas or principles. When you read, let go of tensing up your eyes. . .and your mind. Your eyes can feel soft as they calmly and efficiently glide along the page. It's a good way to develop relaxed concentration.

3. Inconveniences. When the line at the supermarket stalls, when you lose a phone number, when the TV or the toaster self-destructs—such everyday inconveniences can whittle away at your zest for living. Begin with the smaller hassles, such as waiting in line. Let go of leaning forward, holding your breath, frowning, and tapping your foot. These habits create pain, without moving the line a single centimeter. Use the time to relax your mind and body, perhaps by practicing the Easy Steps technique of Chapter One or the breathing patterns described in Chapter Three. You can transform a moment of irritation into a chance to learn something essential to your own well-being.

4. Exercise. Our muscles ache while working out, tempting us to brace against the discomfort. Of course, this added tension only aggravates the pain. Whether you're running, hoisting weights, or doing aerobics, relax every muscle that you aren't trying to develop, especially in your face. Tell yourself, "I'm not wasting energy by fighting this workout, so now the workout is easier." It will be.

5. Temperatures. If you're too hot or cold, your mind may resist the discomfort. Your muscles may tighten, as if to push away the coldness or hotness. Instead, completely accept the temperature, exactly as it is.

This is a subtle exercise, and you may need to experiment a few times before you get the knack of it. When you stop fighting a temperature, it may seem more uncomfortable for an instant, and then it may feel much better. A "too cold" feeling may turn into invigoration, for example.

It may help to neutralize the temperature by thinking of it as just being "energy." We have a whole set of memories and attitudes built up around thinking "I'm freezing," or "I'm roasting." If we think of the feeling as simply an intense sensation, a strong current of energy, it may seem less oppressive. We *can* modulate our own experience.

Of course, you may want to change your clothing or turn on the heater even after you let go, but sometimes that isn't possible. When you can't adjust the thermostat, at least you can adjust your attitude.

Key Ideas from Chapter Four

When we feel distressed, it's usually because we're tying our own happiness to the outcome of some problem. We assume that we can't be happy unless everything marches to the cadence of our own desires. If we realize we can enjoy life even in less than ideal circumstances, we'll escape from the prison house of rigid expectations.

The Art of Letting Go

The Power of Effortless Choice. Choice is at the source of everything we do, and each decision adds its own bit of color to the mosaic of our lives. Yet many choices are made unintentionally. We may discover ourselves finishing a wedge of apple pie that we hadn't noticed we were eating. While thinking of something else, we chose to get up, open the refrigerator, and lift out the pie. Some people are oblivious to over ninety percent of the decisions that set their life's direction. Choice is the silent dictator of destiny, the whisper that's stronger than a shout.

Choice is the source of not only physical actions, but mental actions as well. Without meaning to, we may choose to agitate, frustrate, and depress ourselves. Fortunately, we can choose to release these upsets instead.

In this chapter, you'll learn some strategies for letting go by a simple process of choice. Before learning these methods, it's useful to look more closely at the way we unconsciously decide to feel dissatisfied.

A Self-Inflicted Wound

Unhappiness is easy to come by. We don't have to sit down in the morning and make a list of ways to aggravate ourselves. We don't need books on *The Power of Negative Thinking* or *How to Lose Friends and Alienate People.* Effortlessly and automatically we choose to feel distressed.

We can tell that our upsets are automatic because they're so repetitious. The same old tattered melodramas trudge across the stage, in the theater of the mind. These dramas vary from person to person, but within each individual they repeat themselves with little variation. As we have seen, most of our self-frustrations follow this cycle:

1. The mind encounters a problem or an obstacle.
2. The mind struggles and strains to get the obstacle out of the way, much as if it were a physical barrier.
3. This inner struggle stirs up painful emotions.

Our distress results from step two of the cycle. We make an unconscious choice to struggle and strain. Strain is the critical link between *noticing* a problem and *feeling bad about it.* Tensing up turns problems into pains. Where there is no struggle, a problem becomes more like a puzzle than an irritation. Yet frequently we assume that a problem "makes" us upset, as if we were push-button vending machines: Push the threat button and the machine delivers a frown. Push the no-threat button and a smile dependably materializes.

> Imagine a couple coming into counseling with bruises all over their arms and faces. As they sit down, the husband makes a sarcastic comment to his spouse, and she immediately smacks herself on the cheek. "See what you made me do," she shouts, "how can you treat me this way?" Upon hearing this accusation, her husband promptly pokes himself in the nose. The bewildered counselor learns that they suffer from a shared delusion: "Whenever my spouse says something cross, I have to strike myself immediately."

Now this is bizarre, but what you and I do is almost as startling. When we run into a problem, such as harsh criticism from someone we love, our impulse is to tighten up. This tension hurts our minds as much as a poke in the nose would hurt our bodies. But like the mixed-up husband and wife in the story, we don't see that our injury is self-inflicted. *Our* hands are on the controls.

Admittedly, some unhappiness results directly from our problems. It may be inevitable, for example, to feel hurt when someone puts us down. A putdown stings, like a slap in the face. But like a slap, the sting can fade away in a few minutes. Suppose someone insults me, and therefore hurts me for five minutes. Suppose I then fret about the incident for five hours, hurting myself with mental strain and muscular tension. Who gave me the greater insult, my antagonist or myself?

The Method of Choice

One summer afternoon, while leading a workshop in the San Bernardino National Forest in Southern California, I challenged the participants to list every conceivable technique for coping with unpleasant emotions. "If you were angry, afraid, or sad," I asked, "what could you do to start feeling better immediately?" Soon they had listed twenty-seven alternatives, such as writing down one's feelings on a piece of paper, and then burning the paper. Or, driving to a secluded area, rolling up the windows, and screaming. Or, curling up in a blanket and dunking chocolate chip cookies in warm milk.

There was one solution nobody mentioned, perhaps because it seemed too simple: Choose to let go of feeling unhappy.

Many people don't realize that they can simply choose to let their tensions fade away. Remember, most of our tensions wouldn't even be there if we weren't straining and struggling inside. By *choosing not to struggle*, we can let go of unhappy feelings. Here is an important technique that helps us make this pivotal choice.

———————□———————

Method 16: The Method of Choice

Special benefits: Although this is a subtle technique, it's also one of the quickest. With practice, it may require only a few seconds.

Whenever you're unhappy, locate the feeling of strain and struggle in your mind or body. Zero in on the strain and realize that it's triggering painful sensations and emotions. Then ask yourself, "Would it be *good for me* or *bad for me* to stop straining so much? If it would be good for me, am I willing to let go of straining?" Listen carefully for an answer from within. If the answer is yes, make a conscious choice to let go. Make the choice clearly, gently, and without excessive effort; simply choose to let the straining subside. In summary:

1. Experience yourself straining, creating unpleasant feelings in your mind and body.
2. Ask yourself, "Am I willing to let go of *straining?*" Listen for an answer.
3. If the answer is yes, make a clear and conscious choice to let go.

These three steps follow the pattern described in Chapter Three—tuning in to the tension, preparing to let go, and releasing.

————————□————————

A training session in the Method of Choice. Helene has lived with Rob for two years. They feel essentially married, but Helene jokes with her friends that she's become a "computer widow." Rob belongs to a programming club, and sits up late massaging his software toward absolute perfection.

Helene: The computer widow joke isn't funny any more. I'm really quite resentful.

Chris: From your tone of voice it sounds like you're clearly in touch with your own frustration. Can you feel some strain or struggle inside? (She nods.) Describe what the straining feels like, right this instant.

Helene: I feel sad, and stubborn like I want to grit my teeth. My head aches.

Chris: "Strain" is an attitude that runs through all of those feelings. It's like a harsh, clashing color, woven into a tapestry.

Helene: It wears me out. (Helene is in contact with the attitude of strain, which completes step one of the method. Now on to step two.)

Chris: Would you be willing to let go of straining?

Helene: I'd love to. (That's not the same as "I'm willing to," but I accept her answer and proceed to step three.)

Chris: Make a conscious choice to let go of that strain, at least a little of it.

Helene: OK. (Pauses.) I don't believe I'm completely ready to drop it. I keep thinking, "If I let go, then I give up and he wins."

Chris: Ah! That's why it's good to ask, "Am I *willing* to let go?" But perhaps you can feel better, without letting Rob ignore you.

We worked for another fifteen minutes along the same lines, and Helene dissolved a lot of the upset. Several times she had to stop and ask herself if she was willing to relax. Whenever she realized that she could feel more at peace without giving in to Rob, she immediately felt better. It also helped to release a small amount of the tension at a time. The next day Helene felt comfortable enough to talk to Rob, and he admitted he had "an unnatural relationship with my PC." They made some agreements about spending time together, and eventually Rob thanked her for not allowing the relationship to stagnate.

Having seen how the Method of Choice worked in one situation, let's take it apart, step by step.

Step One: Experience yourself straining, creating unpleasant feelings in your mind and body. *(Tuning into the tension)*

One quick way to tune into the sense of strain is to ask yourself what *emotion* you're feeling. When you examine emotions such as anger, fear, guilt, or sadness, you'll find a powerful tension inside of them, like the nucleus at the center of an atom. You can also find strain in muscular tension, and in the attitudes of pushing and bracing (Chapter Two).

Perhaps the most important syllable in step one is the *ing* at the end of straining. If the method began by saying, "Experience the strain that you feel," strain would sound like a "thing," sitting there cluttering up the mind. But to speak of straining implies that it's not a thing but an inner action. It's something we're doing. It's as if we said, "I've got a problem to solve, so I'm going to frown, squeeze the muscle tissues in my neck, and wish real hard that life was easier." Or, "My boss gave me a bad review, so I'll hold my breath, increase my gastric secretions, and concentrate on how I always get a raw deal. That's bound to help!"

Step Two: Ask yourself, "Am I willing to let go of *straining?*" Listen for an answer. *(Preparing to let go)*

The word "straining" is emphasized to show that we're only bidding goodbye to inner strain and struggle. We are not letting go of intending to resolve our problems, having high standards, or acting responsibly.

It may seem silly to ask if you're willing to relax and feel better.

"Of course I am!" you may reply, "Why else would I be reading this book?" But people have many hidden hesitations about abandoning their distresses. Remember Helene, who thought letting go would mean "losing" in her conflict with Rob.

Furthermore, many people find that confronting the question of willingness triggers an automatic reduction of tension. So ask yourself sincerely if you're willing to let go, and listen for an answer from within. If you decide you're unwilling to give up the tension, then you know it's something you're freely choosing. Sometimes we would honestly prefer to be upset rather than to calm down and relax. But if you are willing to feel better, go on to . . .

Step Three: Make a clear and conscious choice to let go. *(Releasing the tension)*

We create our own moods through a series of unnoticed decisions. These acts of choice are so close to us that observing them is like trying to catch ourselves falling asleep. It's easy to notice ourselves agonizing as we *prepare* for a decision, but the final moment of choice may be almost invisible, like a puff of wind that shifts the direction of a weather vane. Here's a game that illustrates this idea:

> Let's agree that some time in the next sixty seconds you will raise your arm over your head. See if you can catch the instant just before the arm goes up, the instant when you choose to lift it. Try it a few times, and see if you can spot the millisecond when you make the actual choice. This is the almost invisible mental event that triggers all behaviors—lifting a spoon, running a hundred yard dash, dialing a phone call, or whispering, "I love you."

Since the act of choice is as slippery as quicksilver, how will you know if you did let go? You'll know because you can feel the difference. After letting go for a few minutes, you'll notice relief, lightness, calmness, softening, or a sense of resolution. People say:

"It's a 'liftoff.' Something heavy becomes lighter. After a good one, I find that I'm smiling."

"Something settles into place, and I stop holding my breath. It isn't dramatic, but I feel refreshed."

"When I'm mad it feels like junk, and when I let go I don't feel as junky. I want to say, 'Ahhhh, that's better.' "

You might want to try it yourself. Pick some insignificant irritation you've run into recently, and think about it till you notice some negative emotions. Then go through the three steps:

1. Experience yourself straining, creating unpleasant feelings in your mind and body.
2. Ask, "Am I willing to let go of *straining?"* Listen for an answer.
3. If the answer is yes, make a clear and conscious choice to let go.

The first few times, explore the Method of Choice in a quiet place with no distractions. Go slowly, taking as long as you need. Don't worry if it doesn't work perfectly. Instead, concentrate on your successes. Remember whatever helps you create these successes, and try the method with other small problems. (You might use the examples mentioned in Chapter Four—driving, reading, minor inconveniences, physical exercise, and unpleasant temperatures.)

Here are three examples of the Method of Choice in action.

1. The aging father. Wanda is divorced, and her seventy-eight-year-old father Max lives with her. Resenting the aches and infirmities of advanced years, Max takes out his frustrations on Wanda. He makes a great fuss if she wants him to turn down the TV or walk to the corner mailbox. Wanda is straining (1) to stop resenting her father, and (2) to make him the father she'd hoped he would become in the mellow years of retirement.

When Max gets irritable, Wanda speaks to him firmly and patiently. She seems to be doing the best she can, but she keeps straining and pushing for things to get better. She feels irritated, and her headaches have become more frequent.

Wanda finds that she's mainly upsetting herself by struggling to make Max the father she hoped he'd become. She needs to give up the expectation that Max will fit her model of a loving dad.

Interestingly, after she releases tension for two weeks, her father suddenly seems less demanding. When one person relaxes, it's hard for others to remain tense and hostile.

2. The insomniac. Millions of people suffer from insomnia. Angie, for example, is a college student who works full time and studies when she can. She's usually so charged up at the end of the day that she lies awake for an hour or more. Let's imagine we can read a transcript of her thoughts while she uses the Method of Choice to help herself sleep.

I'm straining in all directions at once. I'm straining to go to sleep, straining to solve problems from today, straining about last week's problems, and worrying about how I'll function with no shuteye. Am I willing to let go of all this? (Pause.) What comes to mind is that if I let go of struggling to go to sleep, I won't go to sleep. But it's the struggling that keeps me awake. OK, so I am willing to stop straining for sleep. Now I'm starting to soften out the tension. Good . . . that feels nice. But now look what's happening. I'm getting excited, thinking, "Wow, I'm practically asleep!" and that tricks me into tensing up again. So when I try to relax *in order to sleep,* I wind up tense. When I let go just for the sake of making *this moment* more comfortable, I feel more peaceful.

After a while Angie can feel herself unhooking from the struggle. Ten minutes later, she's snoring.

Other suggestions about insomnia: If you rest in bed with a thoroughly relaxed mind and body, you are already receiving most of the benefits that result from sleep. In fact, a deep meditation may be even more rejuvenating than a snooze. Therefore lying awake at four a.m. is the ideal time to practice the techniques of this book, especially the "relaxers." If your muscles have gotten tight, as sometimes happens during dreams, you may want to get up and drink a little hot liquid or take a few minutes for self-massage. Then practice a technique such as Take a Breather (Chapter One), Word Magic (Chapter Two), Body Release (Chapter Three), or Instant Relaxation (Chapter Nine).

3. The singles mixer. Frank is forty and recently divorced. He's jittery tonight as he walks in the door at his first singles event. Frank is familiar with the Method of Choice, and here's how he uses it:

I feel like heading right back out the door. My hands are sweaty and my stomach's jumpy. My mind is tensing itself, out of the fear that I won't come across OK. I'm wishing I could know that people will like me. It's that old "guarantee" hangup; I've always got to know how my risks will turn out. All right. Am I willing to let go of that? (He chooses to let go.) Well, I still feel the same. Let's go back and focus in on the feeling of strain and tension. I notice the usual frown that says, "I *must* force everything to work out. I have to push and try hard to make this a perfect experience." As I look at what a big deal I'm making out of a little social evening, it's starting to be comical. There—I just let go of a lot of tension without even trying. I'll focus again on how I'm straining. Uh huh. Am I willing to let go of some more? Yes ... Good, good ... OK ... Now I've dropped at least fifty percent of it.

Frank sees a warm-looking woman about his age sitting across the room. At the thought of talking to her, his anxiety surges upward. He stands quietly and lets go again. He still feels shaky, but he's dispersed the worst of it. He walks over and sits beside the woman who caught his eye.

Frank encountered some obstacles, but he overcame these by systematically moving through the Method of Choice. The first time he tried to let go, nothing happened, so he went back to step one. All of us run into hitches in the letting go process, but that needn't be discouraging. It's par for the course.

Let It Be

Let It Be is another "releaser," closely related to the Method of Choice. Generally we become tense when we're fighting or criticizing what's going on in our lives. To feel better, we can declare a mental truce, and stop being so negative. A seminar leader showed me how this works with simple muscle tension. She suggested I find a place in my body that was tight. "My chest is tight," I said.

"Do you want to change the tightness?" she asked.

"Of course."

"Chris, would you be willing to *let go of wanting to change it?*" That was an odd-sounding question, but I had noticed two years previously during the est training that accepting muscular tension usually leads to relaxation. So I stopped trying to make the chest muscles feel differently, and they immediately felt better.

Like the Method of Choice, this is a subtle technique; it may take a while to get the drift of letting something be. But it's a revelation to see what happens when you stop wishing a tight muscle would stop aching: It either relaxes right away, or it stays tense but is no longer bothersome. Either way, you win by letting go.

The same principle applies to anything unpleasant, not just muscular tension. If you're irritated, you may find yourself resisting the feeling of irritation, objecting to it, and wishing it would disappear. But if you just let the *feeling* of irritation be there, neither encouraging nor discouraging it, it will frequently diminish. And of course, we can become more contented if we stop resisting the *situations* in which we find ourselves. If traffic is slow, or a lunch date is late, or there's borscht on your blouse, you can feel better immediately if you decide to let it be. Here's a summary of the method.

----□----

Method 17: Let It Be

Special benefits: Demonstrates the practical value of absolute acceptance.

1. Notice how you're resisting, resenting, disliking, or criticizing a situation, a person, a physical tension, or an unpleasant emotion.
2. Choose to stop fighting it. Put absolutely no energy into wanting it to be any different. It may help to concentrate on something else, and ignore what's bothering you for a while.

----□----

If you need to block out what's bothering you, the next method will help you do that.

Attention Shifting

You can use the power of choice to deliberately pull your thoughts away from your troubles.

----□----

Method 18: Attention Shifting

Special benefits: This is a technique of "positive distraction" that blocks stressful thoughts and feelings.

Focus for a few minutes on a subject that is either neutral or pleasant. Here are four possibilities:

(1) List ten things you're looking forward to. They needn't be important things, just things you'll enjoy—like breakfast tomorrow morning. (2) Slowly count something that's emotionally neutral—leaves on a plant, dots in a square of tile, letters on a printed page, etc. (3) Exercise your memory by recalling twenty things you did yesterday. (4) Take two minutes to think of qualities you like about yourself, giving specific examples of each.

————□————

The key to using this technique is to concentrate on the neutral or positive topics. Your mind may tell you that these are terribly irrelevant things to think about, but that's exactly why they work. Because they are disconnected from your usual thought processes, they interrupt the cycle of distress. After a few minutes of positive distraction, you can re-focus on whatever you need to do next.

At this point you know most of the primary methods of *Feel Better Now*. Chapter Six will show you how to sharpen these methods so they work more quickly and consistently. Pay special attention to the sections on pitfalls and shortcuts.

Key Ideas from Chapter Five

Unhappiness begins with a choice:

1. The mind encounters a problem or an obstacle.
2. The mind unconsciously chooses to strain and struggle against the obstacle.
3. Straining triggers painful emotions, such as anger, fear, and sadness.

Noticing a problem plants the seed of an upset, straining and struggling makes the seed sprout and grow, and stressful emotions are the flowers—or the weeds. It's a handy shortcut to know that almost every distress arises from the same root.

When we aren't pushing against it, an obstacle becomes more like a puzzle than an aggravation. Tensing up turns problems into pains, but letting go turns problems into games. Every time we let go, we add a bit of positive color to the mosaic of our minds.

6

Tips, Traps, and Tricks
A Self-Help Mini-Manual

This chapter is a good place to look when you need special help in letting go. It's a practical mini-manual, a storehouse of specific tools for feeling better rapidly. Let's begin with suggestions for learning to use these tools.

How Should I Practice?

First of all, practice as much or as little as you choose. Some readers of my previous books have benefited without any practice whatsoever. Others have made a game out of these strategies, as if they were learning to play racquetball or bridge. If practice becomes a "should," it may feel like a burden. Remember, no one is likely to master all of the ideas and techniques in this book. It's a smorgasbord; take what you like.

Perhaps you want to practice often, but you haven't much time. In that case, look for an opportunity early in the morning when you don't need to focus completely on what you're doing. Take a few minutes while you're showering, shaving, commuting, or doing errands. If you spend your day with small children, wait until they're occupied for five or ten minutes, or else until nap time.

During the rest of the day check your stress level periodically, and relax enough to take the edge off the tension. Even when your schedule is at maximum intensity there are many potential "body breaks" when you could take a few deep breaths and let the tension evaporate. Let go during low-concentration tasks, such as errands, repetitive work, and non-stressful conversations. Watching television is a fine opportunity. Observe your reactions to every scene and character, and notice when you start straining—tensely trying to force a situation to turn out right.

Finally, as you fall asleep in the evening you can teach yourself to associate certain words and images with relaxation. As you drift off, think of your muscles turning into soft clay or foam rubber. Repeat phrases such as, "I relax deeply and easily, whenever I choose." The more you associate a phrase with relaxation, the faster it will work.

By following these suggestions, you can practice without adding time to your schedule. If you want even faster results, here's what to do:

1. Treat yourself to a leisurely period of unwinding, once a week. Try it as you begin the weekend. Why carry your workaday burdens into Saturday and Sunday?

2. For tough problems that come up repeatedly, try *fantasy practice.* Close your eyes in a quiet room and visualize the problem (the stressful task, the irritating person, the threatening social occasion, etc.). Notice the feelings of pressure and tension that develop. Every time you start feeling bad, release the pressure. Practice for ten to twenty minutes at a sitting, and repeat the process several times. When you're actually faced with the stressful situation, you'll probably be calmer.

One more idea: After you've tried out various techniques, concentrate on using only one or two methods, so you become familiar with them. We need to follow the same steps many times, so that they form an automatic pattern.

Putting It All Together: A Menu of Methods

Having so many different tools for letting go is great, but it can also be confusing. It helps if you divide the tactics you have learned into three steps—focusing on the tension, preparing to let go, and releasing.

Here is a table listing different things you can do in each of these phases. Some of these sequences of steps fit very well together, but don't be afraid to mix and match items as if you were ordering a Chinese dinner.

Three Phases of Letting Go

Tuning In	*Preparing*	*Releasing*
Notice whether you're primarily pushing or bracing. Locate and experience your own physical tension.	Exaggerate the pushing or bracing for a moment, so you can see it's a waste of energy. Notice that it's hard work to be tense. Or: Observe the tension for two minutes, without trying to change it.	Let yourself settle back into balance. Imagine that your muscles are becoming something soft, like clay, candle wax, cotton, clouds, Jell-O, foam rubber, or clear, soothing water.
Feel yourself straining. Ask: What am I straining to do?	Ask: Is straining good or bad for me? Or ask: Is the tension accomplishing anything? Am I willing to let go?	Gently choose to let go, clearly and consciously. Or: Do something constructive instead of just getting tense.
Ask: What am I demanding? What do I think I have to have in order to feel better?	Realize that demanding creates distress.	Change the demand into a preference.

Look back over this list and notice which items appeal to you. See if they'd flow well together. Of course, you can sometimes move from the tuning-in step to releasing, without any preparation step. You can also go directly to the releasing phase, without further ado.

Now it's time for five of the most important suggestions in *Feel Better Now*. Here are two key pitfalls to avoid, and three simple shortcuts.

Pitfalls

When you learn a new skill, you'll inevitably make mistakes. But if you know what to watch for, you can catch these mistakes before they become discouraging. Be alert for the following hazards, as you learn to let go of frustrations.

1. Trying too hard. I once studied a system of self-defense called aikido. Rather than relying on kicks and punches, aikido employs a pattern of flowing, dancelike movements that rapidly immobilize an opponent. Most of these maneuvers are carried out with a minimum of exertion. I remember standing with a practice-partner who was much larger than I am. He was gripping my wrists, and I was supposed to slip free, using a special move. "Don't try to muscle it, Chris," he kept saying, "If you use more than a few ounces of pressure, the technique won't work." I'll never forget the eerie sensation when I finally did it right and he could no longer hold me.

The techniques in *Feel Better Now* are like psychological aikido. In the Method of Choice, for example, releasing tension is a light, effortless action. Why work hard, trying to "force ourselves to relax?" Why strain to stop straining? Why struggle to get away from struggle?

Here's a technique that's good for people who try too hard to relax:

Method 19: Easy Steps

Special benefits: Establishes a small, easily attainable goal, so that letting go happens without trying hard.

> When it seems difficult to relax, deliberately set your sights low, and aim at reducing the unpleasant feelings by a tiny amount. Try it with physical discomfort, to begin with. Locate a tense muscle, and see if you can reduce the tightness, even if the improvement is barely noticeable. Most people can do this with a few minutes of experimentation. Once you reduce the tension slightly, continue to let go of a tiny bit of the tightness *repeatedly*. Take your time, till you have reduced the pressure by roughly fifteen to fifty percent.

You can also use Easy Steps with emotional upsets. Start out by practicing on minor problems, such as a brief traffic delay. Notice how irritated you're feeling, breathe slowly and deeply, and dial down the irritation by just a smidgen.

When we're in a bad mood, we tend to be pessimistic about whether we can let go and relax. Easy Steps acts as an entering wedge for optimism, showing us that we *can* make ourselves less miserable. And if we can deliberately change our feelings once, obviously we can do that again and again and again, whittling down our distresses to a tolerable level. As one client wrote, "This technique convinces me that I can feel better instantly, just by making a decision. I'm not at the mercy of my own negative moods."

2. Concentrating on non-success. People don't learn by trial and error. They learn by trial and success. Whenever you succeed in letting go, remember how you did it. Don't dwell upon failures.

Some people seem to keep score, giving themselves half a point every time they diminish an upset and subtracting fifty points every time they fail. It's far better to praise yourself whenever you do something positive.

Sometimes after using a letting go technique, you may still feel upset. No one can completely program an emotional release; either it happens or it doesn't. But if you prepare the way effectively, it will happen far more often than ever before. Think of the process as a gentle series of experiments. It's a game, not a battle. Some of your experiments won't succeed, and that's not a problem. Don't try hard—try easy!

Stress Reduction and Psychotherapy

Stress reduction techniques and psychotherapy can support each other, but neither one can replace the other. For example, *Feel Better Now* shows how to let go of perfectionistic expectations. If these expectations are rooted in painful childhood memories, you may also want to uncover the source of the problem through counseling. After psychotherapy, unrealistic expectations probably won't enter your mind as often. Therefore, you won't have to spend as much time letting go of them. But even after therapy, stress management techniques are essential. Emotionally healthy people still have tensions and frustrations.

Shortcuts

Now that you know some pitfalls to avoid, here are three short-cuts to accelerate your progress.

1. Let go "just for now." Letting go seems difficult if we think we have to release a feeling forever, so that it never comes back. That would be quite a challenge. Instead, tell yourself that you're letting go "just for now" or "just for one second." That makes it less of a big production. Or ask yourself, "Could I let go simply as an experiment, to see what happens?"

"Just for now" is a simple idea, but it's remarkably effective. It's enjoyable to play with dropping our tension level for a mere millisecond, and to do that again and again. It helps us relax, and it teaches us that we have a choice about our own stress level. This approach is even more effective when combined with the next shortcut.

2. Play the percentages. Some people find that using specific numbers helps them verify their own progress. In using the Easy Steps approach that you read about a few pages ago, you can think of the tension you felt before you started letting go as "100 percent." That gives you a baseline you can refer to later, to see if you're feeling better or worse. Then try releasing just five percent of the discomfort, or even one percent. As you let go, the tension may drop in a pattern like this: 90 percent, 85, 75, back up to 85, 75, 60, plateauing between 60 and 70, then making a quick drop to 40, and so on. A minor tension may drop more rapidly. "Thinking of percentages helps me measure my progress," one fellow explained, "so I notice that I am starting to relax. This gives me confidence that I can relax some more."

Some people prefer to use another benchmark rather than percentages, such as a hot temperature cooling off a few degrees at a time, or a weight getting a few pounds lighter.

If you use this approach, you may discover that *partially* letting go of tension is an important victory. Many people assume they have somehow failed if they don't eradicate every trace of an unhappy emotion. But notice how much better you feel after dropping even twenty-five percent of your stress. And if you take the edge off your tension frequently, you'll feel more alive and vital at the end of the day.

3. Use the power of repetition. To be able to ease tensions quickly, we need processes that work almost automatically. When you come across a method you like, use it over and over so that it becomes a habit. Use it exactly the same way each time, unless there's good reason to vary the procedure. Repeating positive ideas is also valuable, as in the Simple Affirmations technique from Chapter One.

One method for coping with upsets is based entirely upon the repetition principle:

---------❑---------

Method 20: Repeating the Obvious

Special benefits: Quickly clarifies our thinking about a problem situation.

> Two kinds of obvious statements are especially valuable to repeat: (1) "I understand" statements—statements that explain why we have a problem or an unhappy feeling: "Of course I'm feeling anxious—I always feel nervous in a singles bar. Nothing remarkable about that." "My boss is prone to mood swings, and I guess this is just one of those days." "I'm not surprised I had to take the new telephone back. Everybody buys something defective once in a while." (2) "I can" statements. Repeating what we can do to alleviate our problems is empowering and reassuring: "I can remind myself that other people at this party are as nervous as I am." "If my boss is still irritable after three days, I can request a personal conference." "When I get another telephone, I can ask to try it out in the store." You can repeat such statements either silently, aloud, or on paper.

---------❑---------

These seemingly obvious statements are not at all evident to the unconscious mind. As a result, you may need to repeat them over and over, firmly and clearly, so that you hear the message at deeper and deeper levels.

A case study: The sadistic boss. To learn more about the pitfalls and shortcuts we have been discussing, consider an instance in which letting go was very difficult. Jerri worked in the Department of Health, Education, and Welfare in Washington, D.C. A post-election shakeup placed her under the supervision of Rudy, a thin-lipped manager of the old school, long on criticism and short on praise. He continually undermined Jerri with nitpicking complaints. When Jerri tried to let go, nothing much happened. She decided to use fantasy practice, a strategy that works well with hard-core frustrations. At home, she visualized Rudy making sardonic remarks, and practiced dissolving five or ten percent of the anger she felt. Jerri sometimes got discouraged when the frustration wouldn't fade. Even so, she focused on successes instead of failures, and the technique began to work more consistently.

When she was at work, letting go just for now proved to be of special value. It felt good to increase the number of specific moments each day that she felt free from her boss's dominance.

After two weeks, a mysterious shift occurred. When Rudy began to berate her, his words seemed to stay with him, instead of wrapping themselves around Jerri. After that, Rudy's condemnations diminished. Because Jerri had stopped looking frightened, his sadistic attacks were no longer rewarded.

In a few months, Jerri succeeded in being transferred within HEW. "Without letting go," Jerri admitted, "I couldn't have hung in there. I would have bailed out and quit."

Jerri encountered several obstacles, and at times she was troubled by her "failures." But letting go just for now and practicing through visualization resulted in a dramatic change of attitude.

Remembering to Let Go

When life is full of distractions, how can we remember to do what makes us feel better? You'll automatically use some of the ideas and techniques from *Feel Better Now*, just by reading this book. But how can you make them habitual, so that you remember them several times a day? Here are some memory-joggers. Most of them work by setting up a signal that attracts your attention, like a string around your finger, so you remember to sense your own tension and let it go.

Put your watch on the opposite wrist, add or subtract a ring from a finger, or stash your comb in a different pocket or a different place in your purse. Wear something you haven't put on in a long time. Grow a beard, shave your beard, change your hairdo or the place where you part it. Tell yourself that whenever you notice the difference, you'll remember to check your emotional barometer (see Chapter One), and consciously relax.

Make a commitment that whenever the phone rings, you'll give yourself an extra ring to answer it. In that little space you can take a breath and unwind. Let go every time you make a call, or eat the first bite of a meal, or start your car, or sign your name.

A note that says "Let Go" or just "Remember!" will be helpful. Tape it to your desk, a mirror, the refrigerator, or the dashboard of your car. Put it in your wallet, so you see it when you reach for money. Stick a small piece of tape to the top of your steering wheel, or on a doorknob where you'll touch it several times a day. If you keep a calendar, write a message to yourself on every date for the next two weeks, preferably in brightly colored ink. (It's good to write "let go" in the datebook at three-month intervals, so you're reminded of the idea long after you finish this book.) Some people also set the beeper on their watch or the timer in their kitchen as a self-reminder.

After a while you may notice that your reminder no longer stands out. That's your reminder to change reminders.

There are several places you can leave messages that you'll discover several months from now. Write, "Don't forget to relax!" on some sheets of paper, and put them in a recipe box, your glove compartment, the bottom of your purse or briefcase, a stack of magazines, the pocket of a jacket you seldom wear, or with your income tax records, your good china, and your Christmas lights. It's nice to be surprised with a friendly word of encouragement. The last three locations (tax records, china, and Christmas lights) will remind you to relax at a particularly appropriate juncture.

If you're willing to work at it, you can turn a physical object into an automatic reminder, so that you remember to relax every time you see it or touch it. First, think of some association with the object, either logical or whimsical. A steering wheel could remind you to "steer" a course toward contentment. You might think of "combing" out your tensions or using the "keys" that help you relax. Then, attach a physical object to the wheel, the comb, the keys, etc., and leave it there for two weeks. A piece of tape will do. Every time you notice the tape, say something like, "When I touch my keys, I remember to relax." It takes time and concentration to learn to associate the object with feeling better. But once the association becomes habitual, you'll be reminded several times a day to release any tensions that have accumulated.

In the first six chapters, we have covered twenty basic techniques for letting go of emotional upsets. In Chapter Seven, we'll examine the reasons why most people unconsciously *resist* feeling good.

Key Ideas from Chapter Six

As you practice various techniques, you'll encounter certain pitfalls, particularly the tendency to try too hard. "Try easy" instead. Let go just for now, or just as an experiment. Dissolve only five percent of the straining, then five percent more, and so on.

Of course, we'll never use any technique unless we remember it. Deliberate reminders, using the string-around-the-finger principle, are an excellent way to accelerate our progress.

7

Are You Afraid to Feel Good?

When people take classes on coping with upsets, they often discover something curious: They aren't entirely sure they *want* to relax and feel better. On the surface they intend to, but deep down they wonder if it's a good idea. I remember the time that Craig, a customer representative at a computer company, realized he was afraid to relax and let go. We were talking about a blowup he'd had at work, and Craig was beginning to feel easier about it.

"Let's call the tension you were experiencing when you arrived here today 'one hundred percent,'" I told him. "That will give us a baseline. How much is the tension now?"

"It's down to forty percent, maybe thirty percent."

"OK. Would you be willing to let go of some more?"

"Sure. I like the Body Release work we were doing." (Craig went back to experiencing the tightness in his neck and allowing it to soften.) "I'd say it's down to fifteen percent." (Long pause.) "This is funny. It seems like I'm scared to go farther, and my tension is up to seventy percent. Now I'm relaxing again, but it's like entering the Twilight Zone. It feels good—almost a sweet sort of feeling—but I don't know exactly what to do with it."

"You don't know what to do with this new state of mind, and the feeling of not-knowing is triggering some tension."

"Uh-huh, and I'd like to let go of that. I think I need to close my eyes to concentrate." (Pause.) "It's down to about five percent now, but it's strange to be so peaceful."

Other clients have had similar reactions: "If I drop my guard completely, I imagine something's going to sneak up and grab me." Or, "It's as if I have to hold on to five or ten percent of my unhappiness as an 'insurance policy.'"

When an animal has been raised in a cage, it may be afraid to leave. If it walks out through an opened doorway, it may turn around and step right back in. When people venture out of their emotional cages, they often encounter unexpected anxieties. Without their usual tensions, they feel light and unsubstantial. Our tensions clothe us, like a suit of armor or like the glue that holds us together. Some people half-imagine that if they completely relax they will disappear or float away into the ether. The unconscious mind equates letting go with loss of control. Many of us have been convinced since we were toddlers that the only way to get through life is by staying on guard. To release all that tension seems risky.

As people explore the methods of this book, they learn that they can enjoy genuine serenity without vanishing, floating off, or collapsing into a gelatinous blob.

Misery Is Its Own Reward

Besides the fact that feeling completely secure represents uncharted territory, some people honestly doubt that it's a good idea. They believe that becoming extremely happy or relaxed could result in serious problems. Let's examine the four most common objections, using a debate format—first presenting each objection, and then responding to it.

Objection #1. Letting go could interfere with success.

The argument: We all know the saying in sports: "No pain—no gain." For many of us, the times of deepest distress have been growthful periods. We learn by confronting challenges that tax our abilities to the maximum. Without such challenges, we might turn into such complacent do-nothings that we'd never amount to anything.

Several writers have warned that the stress-reduction craze can be carried too far. Hans Selye, author of *The Stress of Life*, speaks of *eustress* (good stress)—the kind of excitement that keeps us tuned and alert. If stress reduction is used to excess, we may start cutting out eustress as well.

Reply: There's nothing wrong with growing pains, such as the ache a yoga student feels while stretching a muscle. We needn't try to achieve a permanent state of trancelike placidity. Instead, we need to let go of making pain into such a big deal. But strain is different from pain. Strain adds pointless distress to the natural distress that's a basic part of life.

Let's take an example. A salesman named Paul has decided to do more cold calling, telephoning potential clients that he's never met. Paul has avoided this task because it involves rejection. People curse at him and slam the telephone in his ear. If he does three times as much cold calling, he's going to feel some growing pains. But he'll feel even more depressed if he starts clenching his neck and dwelling on all the reasons he ought to feel miserable.

When we need to "pay attention," we think we also have to "pay a tension." There's probably no way to eliminate psychological pain, but we can minimize the useless torment we inflict upon ourselves. If you're not clear whether you're experiencing growthful pain or useless strain, ask yourself this: "Do I need to be very tense in order to accomplish this task, or could I do just as well if I were less agitated?"

Objection #2. Letting go could lead to repression.

The argument: Supposedly we can let go of upsets without repressing the upset feeling, but we may be kidding ourselves about that. When a person is angry it's possible to say, "I'm letting go of my anger," and then sweep the problem under the rug. We shouldn't deny our emotions. When we're upset, it's best to handle the problem on the spot. There's no substitute for assertive living.

Furthermore, we need to ask ourselves, "Where does this emotional energy go when we release it?" If we just try to relax and be cheerful, our suppressed emotions will fester inside and then erupt in some other direction.

Reply: Letting go is the opposite of repression. Repression is stuffing an emotion down inside ourselves. Letting go is allowing it to vanish into thin air.

The concern about repression grows out of Freud's hydraulic model of the mind, in which psychic energy was considered similar to a liquid. According to some, if we squeeze this "liquid" out of one place in our minds, it will show up someplace else.

Try making a tight fist, right now, and feel the pain in your hand as you hold the fist tighter and tighter. That pain is real; there's no doubt that it exists. Now open the hand and let it relax. What happened to the pain? Did it go to your little toe? Is it in your left earlobe?

The pain literally vanished. The pain wasn't a thing, that we had to remove physically like a swollen appendix. It was a *temporary state of consciousness*, caused by the way we were holding the hand.

Similarly, we often hold our *minds* in a way that generates pain. When we stop cramping, crunching, and compressing ourselves, the distress goes away. Or think about a candle flame. The flame is real, but when we blow it out, where does it go? If you're angry and you truly let go of the anger, it will vanish into nothingness like a blown-out candle flame.

Admittedly, it is possible to believe you are letting go, when you're actually stifling an emotion. Chapter Nine includes three techniques that should prevent this from happening. But in general, when we smother our emotions we feel heavy, deadened, and turned off. After releasing an emotion, we feel lighter, freer, more open and alive. Releasing is the opposite of repressing.

Objection #3. Letting go could dull our emotions.

The argument: The greater one's experience of pain, the greater one's potential for ecstasy. To be without unhappy emotions would lead us:

> *Into the seasonless world where you shall laugh, but not*
> *all of your laughter, and weep, but not all of your tears.*
> —Kahlil Gibran, *The Prophet*

Such a "seasonless world" lacks the passion that leads to intellectual, literary, and aesthetic breakthroughs. Would we wish that great artists and visionaries were relaxed all the time? Their capacity to feel anger and sorrow enables them to create works that last forever.

Reply: Certainly emotional turmoil is an integral part of life. After a loss, for example, there is a natural process of grief that needs to work its way to completion. Even so, ninety percent of our upsets are caused by psychological nonsense that has no redeeming personal or social value.

People use the fact that upsets are inevitable to rationalize all kinds of illusions. They pretend that oversensitivity gives them a certain nobility, and that the depth of their misery gives life more significance. Certainly going through rough times may help us learn lessons, and may help us discover our true priorities. But there's no need to make a life-style out of habitual anguish.

Objection #4. Being upset helps us influence people.

The argument: It may sound manipulative to say this, but unhappy feelings get results. There are people who don't respond to polite requests; you need to be livid with anger before they'll listen. Every school teacher has students like this. Too much placidity would take the starch out of the passionate emotions that make a big impression on people.

Reply: You don't have to feel bad to act mad. If you want to display your temper to get somebody's attention, you can put on a show of anger. Frown, raise your voice, whip yourself into a fit. You needn't be torn up inside, in order to make yourself look intimidating.

So far in this chapter, we have seen how people hesitate to relax and feel positive, both because it's an unfamiliar feeling and because they imagine it might have harmful results. Now let's consider some other reasons why people hold on to stress. Most of these reasons are unconscious, and are based upon irrational beliefs.

Rewriting Your Old Life Script

A powerful barrier against changing our own personalities is what Eric Berne called the *life script*. Berne, who originated Transactional Analysis, noticed that people live their lives as if they were reading from the script of a drama. One example is the born loser. No matter what opportunities life presents, the born loser will manage to snatch defeat from the jaws of victory.

Most scripts require lots of tension. Therefore when we let go and relax, we are contradicting the powerful pull of the life script. Think about achievement scripts, for instance, such as "Trying To Be Number One." A role like that requires continual exertion. Similarly, how can a Rock of Gibraltar type feel contented and carefree?

Other life plans involve weakness and failure. Some people make a script out of "Waiting To Be Rescued," a theme that involves copelessness, straining, and struggling. (Think how you feel while looking into the distance for an overdue bus.) Becoming happy would contradict the dusty old habit of hoping and moping.

Certain self-images involve heart-rending melodramas. People with melodramatic scripts love to telephone their friends and say excitedly, "You wouldn't believe the awful thing that happened to me this week!" If life is viewed as one long series of crises, letting go is obviously not permissible.

When we contradict a life script, the mind resists. One of my clients who was usually depressed had enjoyed a couple of wonderful weeks. After a while she began thinking, "Well, that's enough good feelings for now. It's time to climb back into my sardine tin where I can be all cramped and smelly again."

If it's hard to get the knack of letting go, ask yourself this: "Suppose I became far more relaxed and happy. How would this contradict my own self-image? How would it change the way I think I have to be?" For further information, see Eric Berne's book, *What Do You Say After You Say Hello?*

The fortress of unhappiness. Many life scripts involve a game called *wooden leg*. People focus on some real or imagined personal handicap and use it as an excuse for not trying: "Don't ask me to do what everybody else can do—I've got a wooden leg." Unhappy emotions make excellent wooden legs. If intimacy seems frightening, we can keep others at a safe distance by being out of sorts. Similarly, depression protects people from the risk of reaching out. A depressed person may say, "I'm feeling too listless tonight to go make new friends." Our feelings can also protect us from an unaccustomed degree of success, effectiveness, or happiness. We are used to a particular range of satisfaction. When we let go so much that we venture beyond the limits of this comfort zone, our mental machinery will try to draw us back into familiar territory.

Worry Prevents Disaster

For a surprising number of people, it's frightening to feel at the pinnacle of health and well-being. They begin to think, "Everything's going too smoothly. Something bad is about to happen." Unconsciously these people assume that being on edge will prevent negative events. They don't believe in relaxing too much, enjoying too much, or feeling too much self-esteem. Pride goeth before a fall; it's better to stay on guard. Some first-class worriers seem to imagine they're holding the entire universe together by the sheer force of their own anxiety. "Momma," in Mel Lazarus' cartoon strip of the same name, is a good example.

Often the fear of joyfulness was learned from our parents. One man was warned repeatedly as a child, "Sing before breakfast, and you'll cry before supper." Mothers and fathers also tell their youngsters, "Don't get your hopes up, because you might be disappointed." (It's rigid expectations that lead to disappointment, not hope.) All of this boils down to the belief that:

"Things go better with tension."

Once in a long while, a time of great happiness is followed by a disaster. But great happiness is usually followed by either more hap-

piness, a neutral mood, or mild unhappiness. Of course, after drawing four aces at poker, the next hand may seem like a letdown. But
enjoying the four aces didn't *cause* the next hand to be a pair of eights.

Guilt-Repellents

Some people are so afraid of criticism that they make themselves
miserable in order to fend off negative feedback. If they put on a
show of feeling guilty, other people will think, "This is a noble individual who is suffering terribly because of an ordinary mistake."
As a result, self-criticism blocks the criticism of others; guilt repels
greater guilt. We learn to act this way during childhood. Grownups
are unlikely to throw the book at a misbehaving child who is already
remorseful.

Similarly, many of us are harshly self-critical in order to seem
morally superior: "Since I'm hard on myself, I must be a refined and
sensitive soul."

Righteous indignation is another excellent guilt repellent. By in-
cisively criticizing someone else's actions, we get to feel smart, moral,
superior, and *right*. There's no need to look at our own faults, when
we see so much evil around us. This may keep us in a state of outraged
agitation, thundering against dumb drivers, greedy corporations, and
corrupt politicians. But would we rather be "right" or be happy?

The Self-Pity Party

Self-pity is nearly as universal as the common cold. It's so easy
to believe that one has a tougher life than other people. Generally,
self-pity is an act, a performance we put on—so heroic, so dramatic,
so sad. One woman referred to it as her wounded bird routine.

People who play the pitiful martyr often deny that they're play-
acting. "How can I be putting on an act?" they may object. "I suffer
in silence." But surely there is nothing so deafening as suffering in
silence. Furthermore, if the martyr is putting on a show, who is the
most important member of the audience watching that show? Obviously it's the martyr. If you present a poor-me performance, part
of you is putting on the act and another part of you is sitting in the
audience dabbing one eye with a hankie.

Martyrs often frustrate themselves by trying to do things they know
are impossible. "If I'd get a gold star for succeeding," they reason,
"surely I'll get a silver star for ineffectually trying."

Letting go is the ideal antidote to self-pity. How can we pity ourselves while we're feeling free and serene?

Pain Entertains

People are entertained by dangers, risks, conflicts, and hassles. This is reflected in the grotesque media violence and the maudlin soap operas to which people deliberately expose themselves. Just as television dramas captivate millions of viewers, real life trauma adds color and intensity to the daily routine.

According to Dr. Paul Rosch, Director of the American Institute of Stress, many Americans carry the love of excitement to an extreme. (*Time*, June 6, 1983, p. 49) They put off work until the last minute for the thrill of pushing against a deadline. Some become hooked on pastimes that could easily end their lives.

Imagine a half-grown tomcat at play. Picture him agitating himself, tearing around an apartment as if the devil were after him, knocking papers about, and leaping off the furniture. A lot of us engage in the same sort of self-stimulation. If we're as smart as the cat, we'll know when to stop chasing our tails and curl up for a nap.

After reviewing all of the advantages of unhappy emotions, it may seem incredible that anyone ever learns to feel better. In fact, people do learn, but we can expect to encounter inner resistance. To our own mental machinery, letting go seems like dying. There is a kind of death involved, but it's the death of pointless fears and behavior patterns. That kind of dying opens the way to rebirth.

Preview of Chapters Eight through Fourteen

From here on, *Feel Better Now* will emphasize *applications*. You'll see how the techniques relate to self-esteem, intense emotions, sensual pleasures, workaday pressures, personal habits, social issues, childrearing, finding a mate, intimate relationships, and more. In the process, you'll learn ten additional methods.

Liking Yourself
It's Easier than You Think

We acquire patterns of straining and struggling at a very early age. Unfortunately, beliefs that are learned when we're young will often persist, no matter how ridiculous. So if we decide when we're barely out of diapers that life has to be hard, it's difficult to shake that delusion.

Most childhood tension patterns involve low self-esteem, so that every challenge becomes a test of our worthiness as human beings. Those who doubt themselves soon become frightened of life.

Theresa's story illustrates the way poor self-esteem can develop. At thirty-eight, Theresa was a respected mid-level executive. Her second marriage was going reasonably well. She dressed tastefully and got enough exercise to be healthy. Yet Theresa felt like a fake. She thought she had become successful only by fooling people into believing she was competent. We reconstructed her life history as follows:

When she was born, Theresa's mother gave her lots of affection. But money was tight, and after a year her mother went to work. Theresa became fussy, clinging, and temperamental. Her mother reacted with irritation and Theresa remembers being frightened of losing Mother's love. By the age of four she would control herself by tightening her shoulders and her chest when the tears of frustration would come.

Theresa's brother, Mike, was jealous of his cuddly baby sister. He'd call her "Ter-cheeza," which she of course considered the most devastating insult imaginable. And in school, Theresa encountered children who had been abused or neglected. Out of their distress, they were often cruel to their classmates.

After years of similar experiences it isn't surprising that Theresa entered adulthood with insufficient self-confidence. Her story is not a tragic tale of deprivation. Yet despite her apparent success, she assumes that she always has to strain for approval and struggle to be competent.

Parents and Other Enormous Creatures

Many of us grew up like Theresa, struggling for approval. In psychotherapy people typically discover that they haven't felt fully accepted by their parents. They haven't resolved such questions as, "Do Mother and Father genuinely love me?" "Do they respect me?" "Will they ever show me their love in the way I would like?"

As time goes by, we project Mom and Dad onto other people, such as friends and spouses. Theresa, for example, treasured her women friends, but she frequently lost them after a terrible blowup. She demanded lots of attention, and spoke bitterly about how "people are so superficial in their commitments." Actually she was expecting each newfound friend to act as a doting mother, to fill up her private inner void. By straining for their love, she drove them away.

We want approval from others, but what we ultimately need is our own self-respect. Fundamentally, we are the ones who deny ourselves acceptance. It's as if two sub-personalities were wrestling with each other inside of our heads. Like a critical parent, one of these personalities may complain that we're disorganized, overweight, shy, or lazy. There's also a sub-personality that receives these complaints. It acts like a criticized child, making excuses and rebelling against the parent, either actively or passively.

To step out of this ongoing battle between Critical Parent and Criticized Child, you can draw upon a different sub-personality. Think about your own smartest, sanest, healthiest side—your own Wisest Self. If you could draw a symbolic picture of the Wisest Self, what would he or she look like? You might draw such a picture now, or close your eyes and visualize this part of your personality.

The picture of the Wisest Self, or some other good-parent image, can help you feel better when you're under pressure.

---◻---

Method 21: The Companion

Special benefits: Feeling the personal presence of a loving companion meets a profound emotional need.

> Imagine that a deeply caring and insightful person is standing beside you, touching you in a reassuring manner, and offering words of encouragement. You listen, perhaps writing down the suggestions. Then you go on with your activities, knowing you can come back for advice and support any time you choose.

---◻---

This technique is excellent for those who have a good imagination and enjoy visualization. A young woman who was suffering from mild depression described her use of The Companion: "My companion is a man in his fifties, with graying hair at his temples. I call him Winston. He's a lot like Walter Cronkite looked when I was growing up. One time I was blue because I felt like I wasn't accomplishing anything in my life, so I closed my eyes and pictured Winston. He put his arm around my shoulder and said, 'Just compare yourself now with where you were two years ago. You're taking classes, you're eating better, and you've started to date again.' He's like a good father, and I feel more confident after I imagine what he'd say to me."

Wishing Makes It Impossible

As we grew up, many of us learned to act as if being on edge is appropriate. In some mysterious way, being habitually tense is supposed to help us get what we want. This tension takes the form of a certain kind of wishing.

"Wishing" is a word with two entirely different meanings. Constructive wishing means that we're planning, preparing, and acting. That sort of wishing is what gets cars fixed, houses painted, and diplomas earned. But when wishing is mingled with tension it turns into a frustrated yearning, a fearful or despondent longing, a pattern of struggle, day after day.

Tense wishing totally blocks the fulfillment of two of our most basic needs. One basic need is to believe we are worthy of love. The other is to believe we are reasonably competent. These have been combined in the acronym, IALAC: I am lovable and capable. Here's how anxiously wishing for something makes it impossible to feel lovable and capable.

Suppose someone acts as if I'm not lovable, and I begin straining to get that person's acceptance. This creates an *inner mental reality* of insufficient love. Since I am tensely struggling for more love, I obviously assume that I don't have enough. It is flatly impossible to feel sufficiently loved while I am wishing and hoping that someone will certify me as an acceptable human being.

The attitude of sufficient love and the attitude of insufficient love are contradictory. The one will drive out the other. The way to absolutely guarantee that we won't feel loved is to sweat and struggle for more love. Every moment spent wishing for acceptance is a moment when we cannot *feel* accepted.

The other aspect of IALAC is the question, "Am I capable?" Suppose I'm not sure I have what it takes to handle some particular situation. If I start straining to make things work, I create a mental reality of "insufficient ability." There is no way for me to feel capable, if at this particular instant I am aching to become more capable.

Struggling for love and competence is almost a physical process. People try to become perfect instantaneously, without going through any intermediate phases. It's like trying to wriggle out of their own skin.

When we look at our thoughts, we may see ourselves making great efforts to be whatever we are not. We repeatedly struggle to hear what cannot be heard, to see what is out of sight, to understand what remains obscure, to feel emotions that are unavailable, not to feel emotions that are vividly present, not to have done what has been completed, and to have already finished what exists only in contemplation. We can feel the body tensing up, trying to make all of this magic come true.

When we wish for something and go after it, we're likely to benefit. But when wishing is mixed with tension, we end up with a sense of lack. Wishing makes satisfaction impossible. Letting go makes satisfaction available once again.

The Self-Criticism Dispenser

Childhood experience may lead us to assume we're unlovable and inadequate. These attitudes are reflected in automatic thought patterns called "negative tapes." Such patterns play themselves in our minds over and over, like a tape recording that repeats when we press the right button.

Negative tapes are especially common when we make mistakes. When you notice a mistake, try this approach:

Re-Evaluating Mistakes

First, let go. Take thirty seconds or so to breathe slowly and deeply or to use some other letting-go technique. Then ask yourself, "Is this mistake *part of a pattern* or is it *relatively unusual?*" Then let go some more.

If the mistake is part of a pattern, you will probably want to alter the pattern. Committing yourself to positive change will make it easier to forgive yourself. On the other hand, if you make a mistake that's highly unusual, why worry about it? It isn't likely to recur, so clean up whatever mess you're in and drop the whole thing.

One day as I arrived at a local college to lead a workshop, I realized I'd forgotten my pencils. As I zipped back to my house I asked myself, "Do I frequently forget to bring what I need to my seminars?" Five or six years previously the answer would have been "yes," but it had been a long time since I'd pulled that little trick. It was frustrating to have to hurry, but at least I realized it wasn't typical behavior.

Perfectionism: The Little Golden Hammer

The mind is a discrepancy detector. We immediately notice when something doesn't match our model of what it ought to be, especially if our egos are involved. Fine-looking men and women confide to their counselors the secret belief that they're actually ugly. On one's own nose, the tiniest pimple may assume the proportions of leprosy.

One way of unlearning perfectionism is to intend to make five small mistakes this week. You can either let these blunders happen or deliberately create them. Take a wrong turn so that you wind up ten minutes late to a meeting where promptness is not essential. Eat a garlic clove in your breakfast omelet. Make a grammatical mistake in front of a friend, without apologizing. Dial a wrong number, and ask for Zeke. Then say, "Are you sure Zeke isn't there? How about Gertie?"

In situations where they can't accomplish everything they'd like, perfectionists become depressed. Parents who are working full-time are in this sort of bind, and so are school teachers. As one sixth grade instructor said, "These kids would learn beautifully in groups of eight, but I have thirty-two. I have to keep reminding myself that this task is absolutely impossible to carry out as I'd wish."

Some perfectionists are afraid to stop criticizing themselves. They're accustomed to keeping themselves on their toes through self-castigation, and they think they would let things slide if they stopped putting themselves down. They're like a horse that's been trained by the whip. If the whip is thrown away, the horse may not respond to more kindly commands. Even so, both animals and humans can learn to obey a gentle, respectful word of correction.

I used to prod myself onward, even when I was already doing fine. While counseling, preparing a lecture, or answering correspondence, I felt as if I had a gremlin sitting on my shoulders, poking me with spurs and muttering, "More, faster, better!" I began to say to myself, *"Relax—you're on the right track."* If I'm on target right this second, why should I strain to do anything else?

Theresa, whom we read about earlier, had terribly high standards. She described her perfectionism as "hitting myself over the head with a little golden hammer." By laying the hammer down, we can finally feel at home in our limited, fallible, and vulnerable bodies and minds.

Supportive Self-Criticism

Because harsh self-criticism is harmful, a few people go to the opposite extreme. They refuse to even admit, "That was a mistake," or "That action contradicts my own principles." Yet sometimes we need to be good parents to ourselves, by correcting behavior that doesn't work. Such corrections need not seem cruel or judgmental.

Think about the difference between these two statements:

> *"You dummy! You left your bike out in the rain again. Everything you own ends up ruined."*

> *"You left your bike in the rain. I want you to do better at putting away your best things."*

The first parent sounded rejecting and discouraging. The second parent was both confrontational and caring.

Ultimately, most self-criticism grows out of caring. Unless you were concerned about having a satisfying life, there would be no reason to worry about fouling things up. If we can experience this caring whenever we're correcting ourselves, we'll feel better and change faster. That's the key to constructive self-criticism.

Self-Love Is Never a Mistake

I have sometimes asked people in my personal growth workshops, "Why should you give love to yourself?" Their answers frequently overlooked the most fundamental reason: We should give love to ourselves for the same reason we water plants and feed puppies. It's nourishing! It helps us thrive and grow stronger.

We humans are so constituted as to flourish with approval and to wither in its absence. Smiles, caresses, and kind words between mother and child, for instance, help both parties thrive and grow. The same is true between friends, spouses, and co-workers. Something similar can take place within the self.

Self-acceptance is *the willingness to support,* *care for, and openly appreciate* the person that you are.

Can you see that this definition of self-acceptance has nothing to do with whether you made some dingbat mistake during the past five minutes? It is always appropriate to give love to yourself, because it is always beneficial.

Here is a very important experiment. Please go through it step by step, completing one step before even reading the next phase of the experiment.

1. Think of something you did very well. (Take a moment to do that, before going on.)
2. As you think about it, give yourself some appreciation for a job well done.
3. Think of a positive quality about yourself.

4. As you think about it, give yourself some approval for having that positive quality.
5. Give yourself some acceptance free of charge, with no strings attached. (Take your time. There's no hurry.)
6. Give yourself some love . . . just because love is good for you.

Look back on this experiment. When was it easy to give the acceptance? When was it hard? If you couldn't give yourself unconditional acceptance, don't despair! This is very, very common in our culture. Just as parents sometimes hold back their approval, we withhold our own self-acceptance. We may support ourselves, but grudgingly. We may embrace ourselves, but stiffly. Why give ourselves crumbs? Why not give ourselves the whole magnificent feast of respect, encouragement, and appreciation? To genuinely like yourself is as beneficial as rain on a growing garden.

Here are some ways to boost your own self-esteem during the course of daily activities.

————————□————————

Method 22: Self-Acceptance

Special benefits: Contradicts the destructive messages of negative tapes.

> Stop for a moment and remember that you need to be good to yourself. Say or think to yourself, "I care about you. Your well-being matters to me. I want to support you, to do what's best for you. I want a good life for you. I'm on your side." It may strengthen the feeling of self-support if you physically touch yourself during this process. Stroking your forehead or simply folding your hands together gives you a non-verbal message that backs up the reassuring words.

————————□————————

You may want to combine the self-acceptance process with the following technique:

————🔲————

Method 23: Your Special Assets

Special benefits: Counters our tendency to put ourselves down. Feeds self-esteem with concrete, positive statements.

Make a list of your own strengths and virtues. You can probably affirm at least three or four of the following items:

Assets

I care about family members.	I understand myself better than I used to.
I want to succeed.	
I'm a good friend.	I can allow myself to have faults.
I help people out.	
I don't make some of the mistakes I used to.	In at least some ways I'm intelligent.
I try to behave ethically and kindly.	In at least some ways I'm attractive.
I've had some success in my life.	In at least some ways I'm talented.

Write your list on a piece of paper, and carry it with you. When you're feeling low, pull out the list and focus on your strengths, thinking of examples of each one. Giving examples is more convincing than thinking in general terms. It helps even more to state the examples out loud or write them down.

————🔲————

In Chapter Nine we'll examine one of the most important aspects of psychological health—the ways we deal with powerful emotions.

Key Ideas from Chapter Eight

A lot of emotional tension results from wanting to be lovable and capable. Life turns into a struggle for achievements and applause. But until we let go of grasping for more, we can't enjoy what we already have.

9

Wings and Galoshes
Coping with Strong Emotions

Rosa came into therapy suffering from both depression and anxiety. She slept poorly, and would awaken with her heart racing. Her eyes looked melancholy, and in the first session she cried a little, apologizing for breaking down that way.

The years had not treated Rosa gently. Her husband had left her, simply vanishing when her daughter was five. Then at eighteen, the same daughter died of a drug overdose. Like many people, Rosa had come to fear and avoid strong emotions. She had been taught as a child to pull herself together, but that wasn't working any more. Even the tranquilizers she'd been taking for two years didn't seem to help. As we will see later on, Rosa learned to face her feelings and throw away her chemical crutch.

Like Rosa, many of us work hard to suppress our emotions, often by using psychoactive drugs. Some people really do need such drugs, to correct their own off-kilter body chemistry. But a huge number of normal individuals take drugs every day, to simulate a conventional, even-tempered personality. They'd be better off if their calmness were real, and not just a facade. And it might sometimes be satisfying to set aside that facade and crackle like a string of firecrackers.

It may sound odd for me to encourage emotional expression, since this is a book about letting go. Aren't we trying to eliminate our upsets so we don't need to fuss with them? Not necessarily. We waste a lot of energy by bracing and pushing against our feelings. Negative emotions, in moderation, are normal and valuable. They're like warning lights, signaling us that we need to handle a problem, or we need to readjust our own attitudes, or both.

It's Only a Feeling

There's a certain tension between respecting feelings as warning signs and dismissing them as irrelevant irritants. In this chapter, we will blend these two viewpoints, thereby combining two rather one-sided approaches. One approach tells us to rise above our feelings. The other urges us to plunge into them, practically drowning in the process. Actually, we sometimes need to slog along in the muck of our gloomiest moods, and other times we need to float above those emotions where they cannot touch us. In other words, we need to own both a pair of galoshes and a set of wings.

When we're upset, we may forget that what we're confronting is *only a feeling*. Feelings "feel" like more than what they are. Our emotional equipment evolved in the jungle, and it's wired up to a basic set of jungle responses. Our souls are stirred by the same impulses that stir the souls of baboons: Fight, or flee, or eat, or mate. (Turn on your television any evening and the issues of fighting, fleeing, eating, and mating will rapidly appear.)

In a frustrating situation, the old animal machinery begins to rev up. It prepares our bodies for dramatic actions that aren't necessary for such everyday challenges as asking a clerk to replace a defective videotape. Our neurological activity while arguing with a clerk may be just as intense as during a confrontation with a tiger. It seems like a tiger, but it's only a vivid experience. A feeling is only a feeling.

Think of your moods as being like a roller coaster. Every time there's a problem, the roller coaster takes a drop and the rider tightens up. The sense of danger is largely an illusion, because most of our lives stay more or less on track. No matter what we do, there is no way to eliminate all of the dips and the unexpected left turns. The question is, will we cringe and cower as we ride out our lives, or will we bounce along with confidence and verve?

Emotional Housecleaning

Resolving emotional problems is like cleaning house. We start with the obvious messes. We sweep the corner where spiders have created a cobweb metropolis; we round up the dirty socks and bluejeans. Once these preliminaries are out of the way, we notice the handprints all over the front door. It's as if the house continually presents us with the next most important item to handle.

Psychological growth takes place in much the same way. Typically a person comes into therapy because of a major setback. The marriage has ended, and life is in turmoil. The supervisor has written a third warning, and the next step is dismissal. Such pressures goad us into asking for help. As therapy progresses, we notice that we have problems with self-esteem and assertive communication. In cleaning up those issues, we discover unfinished business with our parents. The mind keeps showing us our next priority for improving our lives.

There is one important difference, though, between cleaning house and cleaning up the mind. Because the mind is full of places that we can't see directly, psychological housecleaning requires bringing to light what isn't obvious. We must go on garbage-collecting expeditions, and bring boxes of refuse up to the living room where we can sort them out.

The "rise-above-it" approaches to personal growth, such as positive thinking, occasionally ignore the necessity for sorting out the garbage. They sometimes imply that if we bring in lots of beautiful new thoughts, and don't dwell upon our old, musty attitudes, the latter will disintegrate and fall away. Sometimes they do, and sometimes they don't.

To change the metaphor, think of your emotions as a river. One way to know the river is to sit on the bank, clean and dry, watching the torrent rush by. Another way to know the river is to dive in and hurtle downstream. Some say we should always sit up above the river, as if it would hurt us to go for a swim. Others preach that "the only way out of our distress is through it." They advocate plunging into the flood of emotion, without teaching people to climb out for a while and rest.

How to Prevent Repression

Temporarily ignoring an emotion may be a good survival tactic, but chronically blocking emotions isn't healthy. Here are three ways to bring our feelings to the surface, so we can deal with them constructively. These techniques take longer to use than just a few minutes, but they're an important complement to our quick-relief strategies.

1. Listen to the feeling. In listening to a feeling, focus your mind right in the middle of the hurtful emotion, and imagine that it can speak. Ask the emotion, "What are you trying to tell me?" "What would take away the frustration?" or "What's the biggest thing bothering you?" The reply may be a statement such as, "I don't trust this person," "I can't stand being so hurried," or "That fellow is mad at me."

Sometimes it's important to let our emotions speak to us vividly. Vivid experiences motivate us to take necessary actions. Quentin, for example, had been working long hours for several months. As he talked about this in counseling, he saw how terribly burned out he was becoming. "This is scary," he said. "I guess I feel more strongly about my job pressures than I realized. Now I simply *have* to make a change."

Quentin was able to diminish the burden of his work. He believes that if he hadn't discovered how strongly he felt about it, he would have stumbled along until he collapsed.

2. I feel and I want. Say a series of sentences to yourself, each one beginning with the words "I feel" or "I want." For example, "I feel sad that I forgot to call Ralph. I feel warmly toward him. I want to telephone him before he leaves his office, and apologize." It is best to make these statements out loud or to write them down. That way they will be more specific.

NOTE: We often say "I feel" when we actually mean "I think." "I feel that my boss isn't fair," is a thought about the boss, but "I feel *angry* because my boss isn't fair," identifies a feeling, and therefore fits this exercise.

Approach the experience with an attitude of curiosity. Be patient and receptive, and note every emotion and desire as it comes, big or little, logical or ridiculous. It's a process of discovery—the exact opposite of repression.

3. Put them on paper. It's remarkably useful to simply write down our feelings and thoughts. When I use this technique in classes, people often achieve surprising insights about some dilemma they've been wrestling with for years. Here's an example of what one person wrote:

> I've applied for a job, and I'm more afraid I *will* get it than that I won't. Why is this? The fellow I'll be supervising comes to mind. He talks circles around people, and I'm afraid he'll end up managing me.

The co-worker's glibness was a clearcut hazard that could be handled through specific actions. When the feeling involved a vague, general nervousness about the job, it was impossible to know where to look for a solution. Writing down thoughts and feelings clarified the key issue.

It's valuable to listen to our feelings, and it's valuable to let them go. Emotional health involves a zigzag pattern, moving back and forth between emotional exploration and release.

It's often wise to alternate these strategies. If we haven't done much letting go for a few weeks, we might set aside time to release some upsets. And if we haven't done any emotional housecleaning for a while, perhaps we should deliberately draw our feelings to the surface. Feelings no longer need to frighten us, whether we're analyzing them from afar or plunging into the midst of them. They are our teachers, not our masters.

Overwhelming Emotions

Sometimes a person becomes so distraught that feeling better seems impossible, and those are the times when it's most essential. It may help to tell yourself, "I'm in a tough spot, so relaxation is a top priority," or, "It's going to take everything I've got to pull through. I'd better not waste energy on excess tension."

We almost never give ourselves enough TLC during these rough periods. Instead, we take half-hearted measures, such as watching more TV, snacking on chocolate, compulsively shopping, or drinking to excess. But here are some *positive ways to handle overwhelming feelings:*

- Lie down and listen to soothing music.
- Take a long walk in a beautiful place.
- Enjoy a warm bath.
- Ask a friend for verbal support or physical affection.
- Watch a hilarious movie.
- Watch a sad movie. (Bring tissue.)
- Fully surrender to the unhappy mood. You may want to do this for a specific time period, such as an hour.
- Put fresh flowers in your favorite vase.
- Nap.
- Meditate.
- Pray.

Remember that emotional tension creates muscular tension. A professional massage can open up the tight places, and your troubles may not seem so insurmountable afterward. Hard exercise also helps, as does doing something that takes your mind completely away from your difficulties. And of course, deep relaxation is a profoundly healing, rejuvenating process. Here's one way to achieve such relaxation.

------□------

Method 24: Instant Relaxation

Special benefits: A flexible technique that can be used either brief-ly or for longer periods.

> *Fifteen-minute version:* Sit or lie down with your eyes closed. Count backward slowly, using the following sentences: "Three—I am ready for rest and relaxation. Two—With every breath, I let go and relax more deeply. One—I am now completely open to rest and relaxation." Then go through your body and release the excess tension in (1) your legs and feet, (2) your arms and hands, (3) your torso, and (4) your neck, head, and face. For the rest of the time, slowly repeat some soothing statement such as, "I relax when I need to, I keep my stress level down, and I take good care of my mind and body."

> *Three-minute version:* You can use this technique for shorter periods after practicing the long version at least ten times. After that much practice your mind will have learned to associate the technique with rest. Therefore you'll start feel-ing calmer, and perhaps sleepier, as soon as you count down from three to one. Because this technique causes drowsiness, don't use it when alertness is necessary.

------□------

It's good to become familiar with this method even before you run into a crisis. That way the Instant Relaxation process will come naturally when you need it the most.

Returning to the subject of overwhelming emotions, let's talk specifically about five of them.

1. Rage. Intense anger triggers so much energy that it's helpful to discharge it physically. A person who is angry usually wants to hit or to kick, and psychotherapists have debated about whether it's appropriate to express anger that directly. Carol Tavris in *Anger:*

The Misunderstood Emotion argues that ventilating rage does not lead to discharge. Instead, she says, the anger will grow.

Dr. Tavris and other writers are offering a useful corrective to the extreme emphasis on emotional catharsis of the 1960's and early 1970's. Influenced by the human potential movement, thousands of men and women attempted to recover the feelings they had learned to avoid. This was exciting but it wasn't always practical. When people showed anger, they sometimes alienated friends. When they recovered sadness, they sometimes got stuck in perpetual self-pity. The revolution of reawakened emotion bumped into obstacles, and fell short of its goals.

People don't seem to go to such extremes if they combine the expression of emotion with learning to let go of upsets. In one group therapy session, for example, a fifty-year-old man named Omar brought up his hostility toward his ex-wife. He believed that she had hurt him and gotten away scot free. I asked him to imagine that she was sitting in front of him, and we used a pillow to represent her. Omar talked to her bluntly. As his anger increased, we gave him a soft cloth bat for hitting the pillow. He struck it vigorously for three or four minutes. When he was done, I emphasized that I wasn't encouraging violence or verbal abuse by suggesting that people act out such things in fantasy. Then we ended the session with a relaxation process. A few days later, Omar told me he had been feeling tremendous relief, as if he could finally breathe easily while thinking of his ex-wife. I spoke with him during the next year and found no evidence of any relapse into his excessively bitter feelings toward his wife.

Striking Out Exercise. If you want to try a similar approach, begin by affirming that you will ventilate your rage in a way that does not hurt you or other people. Then use a soft target that won't be damaged by your aggression. A large, well-made pillow is ideal. You may need to put the pillow on a padded surface so as not to bruise your hands.

Warm up slowly, hitting the pillow with medium force until your muscles have loosened up. (If you have a physical problem or if you're out of shape, consult your physician before carrying out this exercise.) Exhale your breath sharply with each blow. Imagine that each impact is diminishing the angry energy in your body and that every sharp, explosive exhale is also expelling energy.

2. Anxiety. Anxiety involves both mental and physical tension. The word "anxiety" comes from a word that means "narrowing," and there's usually a literal narrowing in the chest and throat. It may be hard to get enough breath.

Many people suffer terrifying episodes known as anxiety attacks, sometimes as a result of physiological problems. The attack poses two different challenges. First, there is the feeling of anxiety that is somehow generated in the victim's body. Their hearts pound, their knees shake, and it seems as if they're about to die—but nothing dangerous is happening. Second, people tend to resist the anxiety. They become afraid of the fear, and this is where letting go can help. Instead of fighting the experience, like a drowning person fighting the water, they learn to relax and float with it.

Kate had been having bouts of anxiety for several months. She began to avoid going out in public, thinking an attack might become so intense that she would begin screaming. With the help of a therapist, Kate learned to treat each attack as nothing but a temporary physiological event. She would talk to herself in this manner:

"I can feel the terror in my chest as if I'm choking. I can hardly breathe, but the worst thing that could happen is that I'd pass out, and then I'd breathe automatically. I'll sit on this bench and let go of tensing myself up against the dread. That's a little better. The feeling is still there, but I don't have to make it worse by fighting it."

In time, Kate's symptoms began to diminish and eventually they vanished. This happens to many people, but no matter how long the attacks persist, it's better to float with them than to struggle against them.

3. The fear of death. Some people are terrified of death, while others are virtually free of such apprehensions. Even older men and women who don't believe in an afterlife may be at peace about their own mortality. This implies that an extreme fear of death is a habit of mind rather than an unchangeable instinct. Since it's just a habit, it can at least be moderated.

A man in his early forties had a brush with death that stirred up considerable anxiety. Noticing a change in a mole, he went to his doctor, who removed it. It turned out to be melanoma, a potentially dangerous form of skin cancer. He caught it at an extremely early stage, so that the odds of complete cure are virtually one hundred percent. But even so, it was an unsettling experience.

After receiving consistent feedback from several specialists, he realized he was safe—as safe as any healthy human being can be. In the meantime, it was helpful to transmute worry into practical action. When he started getting nervous, he would use the energy of that fear, saying to himself, "I WILL cut down on fat in my diet. I WILL eat more fiber. I WILL cut my risk factors every way I can." Perhaps by living such a healthy life, he'll survive to the age of 110. If so, that little black mole did him a great big favor.

Often the fear of death results from straining to make life turn out right. People regard their lives as if they were projects, courses of study, sports competitions, or buildings to be constructed. These metaphors imply that one either will or will not "finish it up right," and death is a threat to these plans.

Death is just one phase in the process of living, and each phase involves letting go. As the Reverend Charlotte Shivvers put it in a recent sermon, "We have to give up the delicious dependence of childhood to have an independent self; and we have to let go of part of the independent self each time we enter into a close relationship. That supposedly independent self is still a difficult stage for me to release.... As I flip my reading glasses back and forth here, I'm reminded of another 'stage of life' that I will need to let go, and that is the almost perfectly functioning body that has been mine for fifty years. And, of course, our ending years are a time of letting go to be with death, the final stage of life."

4. Grief. In grief, the mind strains against reality, pushing and bracing against the blunt fact of what has happened. If our grief could speak, it might be saying, "It can't be true! I can't have suffered such a loss. It's a dreadful mistake." When I learned that my own mother had terminal cancer, it seemed as if every nerve and muscle of my body wanted to shout, "No!" One may need to strain against reality, "shaking one's fist at the heavens" for long hours. Later, deep breathing plus relaxing words and images can help melt away the tension. Remember, after a major loss, you need all the energy you can muster. Don't waste it by holding your breath or clamping your jaw.

Denial is a normal part of grief, but many people get stuck for years in unconscious denial. Rosa, for example, had been living in the denial stage during the nine years since her daughter, Carmen, had died of a heroin overdose. In a counseling session, she looked at the ways in which she was still struggling with this event. She realized she was (1) straining to understand why her daughter had become an addict, (2) straining to know whether she could have prevented the tragedy, and (3) straining against her daughter's death having happened.

When I suggested she let go of straining for the tragedy never to have happened, Rosa hesitated. "It's hard to understand, but I feel like I ought to keep fighting against Carmen's death. If I stop fighting against her death, then *she really will have died.*" Tears came to her eyes. "I guess I've just been hiding from the truth."

Other things that helped Rosa release her daughter included using the Seven-Eleven breathing technique, nurturing her body through self-massage, and a form of fantasy practice in which she would do some letting go while visualizing her daughter. In time, she felt a new clarity and serenity.

5. Depression. One may question whether letting go of tension can relieve depression, because a depressed person doesn't seem to be forcing or pushing. Yet many cases of depression are caused by buried emotions—anger, for example. Anger is an active emotion that usually contains lots of tension. Suppressed sadness can also result in depression, and as sad people talk one can hear the strain in their voices. When they let go, both the strain and the sadness diminish. So in all negative emotions, including depression, tension plays a central role.

One effective response to depression involves bringing suppressed feelings to the surface. Then you can start letting go of whatever stresses you've uncovered. On the other hand, depression is sometimes due to a biochemical disturbance. A depression may be biochemically based if:

- The depression came "out of nowhere." It did not result from real-life frustrations.
- If life improves, the depression doesn't lift.
- The individual feels just as blue in the company of close friends and loved ones.
- A sense of humor is almost totally absent.
- There are serious disturbances in sleeping, eating, or sexuality.

In such cases, certain kinds of drug therapies can restore normal functioning, and counseling can also be useful. The techniques of this book may have limited effectiveness against such a disorder, but they can be very helpful against the milder forms of depression.

We've considered some hard subjects in the last few pages. Stop and check your own "tension barometer" to see if your body is feeling tight, or if there are emotions you need to experience and release. It's important to confront harsh realities, but we also need to be kind to ourselves, to allow time for healing and self-nurture.

With all of the emotions we've discussed, you can use both wings and galoshes, sometimes soaring above your own experiences, and sometimes slogging through the thick of them. In either event, you'll move along faster if you know how to quickly dissolve your tensions.

Now, for a change of pace, Chapter Ten will show how letting go can help us feel even better when we're already feeling terrific.

Key Ideas from Chapter Nine

We often treat our emotions as if they're threatening to eat us up. But anger, sadness, and other distresses only seem to be dangerous. They're like transitory mindstorms. If we brace against them, they beat upon us more relentlessly, but if we accept them they will pass away on their own.

10

Are We Having Fun Yet?
Reflections on Leisure & Pleasure

The pursuit of happiness can be a strenuous endeavor. Our leisure time activities often create more stress than they relieve. Let's see how we can find genuine satisfaction during periods of recreation and sensual pleasure.

Working Hard at Feeling Good

A weekend at the seashore. Al and Carrie and their two boys leave one Saturday in June for the Delaware shore. The traffic out of Washington, D.C. is heavy, and there are several bottlenecks before they finally arrive. Al's been at the wheel, muttering about "crazy drivers" and "asinine detours." The family tosses their suitcases onto the motel room beds, jumps into swimsuits, and sprints to the beach. Al can't decide where to park the beach blanket, and finally they find a place to plop down. He has been anticipating this weekend for a month, but every ten minutes he glances at his watch as if he's still in a hurry.

Al's mind has been expecting an experience called "having fun." Now that he's gotten himself to the having-fun place, his mind looks around quizzically as if to say, "I'm here. Where's the fun?"

Often we expect something to be pleasurable because it's labeled "recreation." But feeling good requires a combination of mood, events, and attitudes. If we go on vacation we can expect a change of scene, and perhaps a slowing of the pace. But we can't assume that we'll have fun.

People often treat positive experiences as something to be consumed, collected, counted, inhaled, or eaten. Such pleasure-disorders are similar to eating disorders; in a sense, the *mind* overeats. There's an underlying anxiety about not getting enough. Some people seem to keep score, as if they're building cumulative lifetime pleasure-point totals. Perhaps you have seen the bumper sticker that says, "The one who dies with the most toys wins."

Perfectionism about pleasure is also a curse. Extra-special occasions can make us anxious because we want them to be flawless. In weddings the bride and groom are sometimes devastated because of some trivial gaffe. They're blessed with a sunny afternoon, loving friends and relatives, and a lifetime of companionship in the offing—and the bride sulks because the car bringing the flower girl blew a water pump and they had to start without her.

I remember going to hear a legendary jazz musician and griping because the view wasn't perfect, and the folks at the next table were talking all the time. The music was so intoxicating that one chorus would have given me enough to remember for a lifetime. But instead of enjoying what was there, I was struggling to make it better. The world offers us a thousand times as much potential pleasure as we can possibly absorb. It's an endless feast, a harvest of stimulations. Yet we scramble for more, as if life presented us with scarcity instead of bounty. As a friend once said, "Hell is putting everything outside of yourself—and then grabbing for it desperately."

Part of our greed results from the exaggerated image of happiness displayed by the mass media. Politicians and movie stars wear great big grins, and people imagine that these successful people feel:

> Constantly positive.
> Highly stimulated.
> Cheerful and friendly, regardless of circumstances.

Some people bubble over like champagne, all day, but most of us aren't quite so effervescent. Perhaps it's even misleading to speak of happiness as a proper goal of life. The word "happiness" has a jazzy, upbeat sound to it, but people can feel wonderful without being particularly upbeat. *Well-being* might be a better word to describe what we deeply desire. Well-being is a healthy, centered, positive frame of mind, a comfortable feeling that fits lots of situations in which ecstacy would seem incongruous.

The milder forms of pleasure are as valuable as the more highly activated states. In fact, they may even be more pleasurable, in their own subtle way. Many of us have become accustomed to such intense stimulation from television that we don't even notice the gentler satisfactions. Let's not ignore the feel of a cool breeze, a smile from a grocery clerk, or the steady companionship of a faithful spouse. Joy might be compared with lively music, but well-being is like a silver flute. Joy is a brilliant color, but other good feelings are like pastels. Joy is like a spectacular sunset, but other feelings are like the first evening stars.

How Pleasure Turns On Tension

Sometimes we become anxious because we're afraid our pleasures won't last: "I wish this night could go on forever." "How sad that summer will soon be over." "Well, here goes the last bite of cheesecake." We want to put a fence around good feelings, so they won't go away. But life is a swirling kaleidoscope, not a frozen snapshot. By struggling to hold on to a feeling we crush it, or at best we end up with a stale good feeling.

Pleasure may also make us anxious because we don't believe we deserve it. And even if we feel OK about this present moment, we may be worrying about the future: "My husband and I are so close tonight. I hope we don't go back to being distant later on."

Here's something you can try when you're in a good mood and would like to let that feeling expand.

Method 25: Opening Up to Pleasure

Special benefits: Helps us embrace our satisfactions, without grasping them or trying to control them.

> Take a moment to enjoy what you're experiencing, and then check to see if any tension is diluting your happiness. Allow the tension to soften, and allow the pleasure to gradually expand while you take a few slow, deep breaths. It may help to tell yourself, "I have a right to savor this moment" or "There are always problems, but here and now I'm doing just fine."

A retired police officer used this strategy in dealing with his new-found leisure time: "I'd be puttering around with the old Buick I'm restoring, and I'd feel guilty that I wasn't doing something important. So I'd stop and bring back that nice easy feeling I have when I'm working on the car. Then I'd tell myself, 'Look, buddy, you earned this time,' and I'd go back to sanding the fender."

When you're feeling good, you may be able to feel even better. There's no need to make it a duty or an effort. Just experiment with allowing unnecessary tension to fade, and allowing satisfaction to fill you up inside. In good times or bad times, keep letting go, and enjoy each shift of life's kaleidoscope.

How to Turn Fun into Drudgery

It's not at all difficult to turn recreation into a burdensome chore. One way to do this is to tell ourselves we have to spend our leisure hours in certain ways. When something delightful becomes mandatory, it accumulates a sort of duty-dust that dulls its luster. "I want" turns to "I should," and then to "I must." The second step is to schedule recreation quite rigidly and make a fetish of doing every bit of it. This sets up some marvelous ironies such as running a red light while hurrying to yoga class. We mustn't miss a single minute of this precious opportunity to relax.

Let's not leave any transition time between our activities, either. That way we'll feel rushed and not fully present.

Finally, besides making pleasure a duty, scheduling it, doing it perfectly, and rushing into it, we should push ourselves to do lots of what we enjoy. More is bound to be better. We need to walk farther along this beautiful trail, we need to see every painting in the Louvre, and even though it's ten p.m. there's time for another dessert. But why do we feel frazzled when we're having so much fun?

Straining to Feel Good about Success

Have you ever wished you could feel more enthusiastic about your own victories? After a triumph, people are often unsatisfied. Perhaps they aren't sure they deserve to be successful.

Psychologist Pauline Clance has written about the Imposter Syndrome, the belief that one has succeeded in life only by fooling other people. (*Amtrack Express*, June 1985, p. 51) Theresa, whom we read about in Chapter Eight, is a good example. Some therapists estimate that fully half of all talented people periodically feel as if they've been faking it.

As est founder Werner Erhard has pointed out, the exhilaration from a long-awaited triumph usually lasts about two weeks. Even though a person may have gained an Olympic gold medal or the presidency of a corporation, the mind will take the victory for granted once it has been accomplished. It seems as if after all those years of preparation we ought to spend more than a few weeks being thrilled with ourselves. Frequently, though, it isn't that way, and we might as well let go of grasping for an attitude we no longer possess. Sometimes after we let go of reaching for it, the victorious feeling returns to our minds, effortlessly.

After the hour of triumph has passed, we may find that success is stressful. A major breakthrough changes our lives, and change is unsettling. Some of the most stressful items on a psychological test called the Holmes-Rahe Life Change Scale are positive—retirement, pregnancy, marriage, or even marital reconciliation.

For a hilarious story about the way success put a writer's life into turmoil, read Dan Wakefield's book, *Selling Out*. In one scene the writer, Perry Moss, sits for the first time in a Director's Chair.

> *All eyes were on him as he went to mount the chair that had his name on it, and suddenly it seemed a challenge. It looked storklike and flimsy on its crossed toothpick legs. Bravely, he seized the arms as if he were going to mount a wild bronco, hefted himself up and onto the canvas seat, teetering only slightly, silently saying a prayer of thanks as he opened the large notebook that held the script and pointed his nose down into it, pretending to focus on the swimming words.*

To enjoy a victory, we can let go of struggling to deserve our success, struggling to have more of it, and struggling to adapt to new circumstances. Releasing these useless tensions allows us to find the satisfaction we've worked so hard to achieve.

The Hesitation Step

Most grownups have forgotten how to play. They seldom allow their own spontaneous impulses to propel them forward, tumbling into fun and fantasy. Many people refuse to cut loose without the special permission implicit in a holiday or a party. Or they may use alcohol to allow themselves to act a little goofy. When they buy a drink, they buy a license to let down.

Letting go is a more natural way to slide past stiffness and hesitation. By abandoning the struggle to control everything, we can recover the playfulness we once had as children.

Would you feel free to do these things with your friends?

- Tell whimsical jokes and use far-fetched puns.
- Tease someone in a friendly way.
- Tickle someone.
- Hug a friend impulsively.
- Mock-wrestle.
- Wear outrageous clothing.
- Play a harmless practical joke.
- Dramatically recite a poem.

When you're alone, could you:

- Put on music and dance.
- Imitate a rock guitarist in front of the mirror.
- Have fun with clay, crayons, paints, or poetry.
- Play with your children's toys.

If you let yourself be childlike, what inhibiting thoughts and feelings surface? What would it be like to let them go?

Food: Savoring It without Overdoing It

If you want to experiment with deepening your capacity for pleasure, try it at mealtimes. The principles that expand your enjoyment of a good meal will also help you appreciate a painting, a game of cards, a concert, or a conversation.

The average individual probably experiences no more than fifteen bites out of a typical full-course meal. That's not a major tragedy, but why splurge on a special dinner and get as much benefit as if you've been munching a hot dog?

Furthermore, many people don't eat the meal—they eat the menu. In other words they relate to the *concept* of their food, rather than the way it tastes. They'll say, "I just love these scallops," yet their flat tone of voice conveys no satisfaction. They know they usually like scallops, so therefore they must be having a tasty dinner.

Pleasure is less dependent on the dish itself than on the *interaction between ourselves and the food*. We've all had times when the setting was ideal, our mood was right, and we were "listening" to what we were eating. At those moments, something as simple as cheese and a chunk of bread becomes a memorable delight.

Paying attention to the true taste of the food can keep us out of the *expectations trap.* We sometimes develop rigid expectations about how an omelet, a cheeseburger, or a cabernet sauvignon is "supposed" to taste. If what we're consuming doesn't fit these criteria, we refuse to enjoy it.

Our expectations usually increase when we put lots of effort into planning and preparing an event, which is why spontaneous pleasures are often the best. Expectations also increase when we have already had a similar experience that was fabulous. When the first meal in a particular restaurant is dazzling, the second almost never seems as good. And finally, cost is a factor. It's said that we get what we pay for. We also *expect* what we pay for, and there's the rub. When we spend lots of money for a fancy dinner or a classy auto, we run a risk of being disappointed. The way out of this trap is to change our demands into preferences. We'd like the meal or the car to be sensational, but if it's not, we can enjoy it for what it is.

Awareness of what we're eating also helps us dine more moderately. As one woman told me, "I used to wolf down a couple of donuts while I was worrying about my bills or my kids. Then I'd want another, because I hadn't enjoyed the first two. Nowadays I notice every bite—and I pause between them. I've stretched a tiny chocolate truffle out to fifteen minutes, and I loved it!"

Those who can thoroughly savor their pleasures tend to create value out of an experience. If we ask ourselves, "How can I create something good for myself, here and now?" we'll be on the right track. Usually the best way to create value is to relax and release our tensions. Whether one dines upon Beef Wellington or bean burritos, letting go is the entree to maximum enjoyment.

Letting Go in Bed

One of the enchanting things about sex is that it's effortless—unless the mind turns it into a Major Production. Sometimes it's complicated to decide when, where, and with what safety measures, but once that's out of the way there is seldom any reason to feel uncomfortable... except for the clankings and groanings of our mental machinery.

Both men and women are ambivalent about losing control at peak sexual arousal. We try to make it happen (because it feels so good) and to keep it from happening (because it's so scary).

Performance anxiety is another problem. If you've seen Woody Allen's movie *Everything You Always Wanted to Know About Sex*, you may recall the scene in which the faltering hero is attempting to consummate matters in the back seat of a tiny sports car. The episode becomes a feat of engineering that rivals the construction of the Eiffel Tower. It's such a Catch-22: "If I don't worry about having an erection, it will be there. But if I do worry, it might not be, so I had better worry about whether I'll worry about it, but that fouls things up too, so I'd better. . . punt." Struggling for control leads to lack of control.

Similarly, if a man having intercourse pushes *not* to have an orgasm, the tension may trigger the orgasm more rapidly.

Women are able to have intercourse even if they're trying too hard, but they may still be blocking their own excitement. Kathleen, for example, came to therapy because it was hard for her to relax and enjoy sexual intimacy. (One may think this problem went out with high-button shoes, but it's not terribly uncommon.) There were no major conflicts between Kathleen and her husband Jeff. It was just hard for her to stop anxiously grasping for pleasure. Let's imagine we can tune into her thoughts during lovemaking, both before and after she had some practice in letting go.

Before learning to let go, Kathleen thinks:	After learning some ways of letting go, Kathleen thinks:
I can feel myself closing off as he puts his arms around me. The neighbors are playing jittery music on the radio, and that distracts me. I can't find a comfortable position. My arm keeps getting in the way and I make a joke about how I wish it could bend in the other direction. I'd better act like I'm enjoying this. I don't want him to know that I'm tied up in my thoughts and fears. Now I'm starting to feel a little pleasure in my body, but when I reach for it, it slips away. Jeff sure is enjoying himself. I resent the fact that this is all for him. But I'd feel humiliated if he knew that my moans and sighs are nothing but a performance. What's wrong with me?	Uh-oh. I'm afraid I won't be able to enjoy this. So what's going on? (She observes the feelings and thoughts that pass through her mind.) I think I'm trying to *make* myself feel all Hollywood-romantic, instantly, instead of warming up slowly. I can let go of trying to act like a tigress in heat and accept whatever I do feel. (She allows the tension to soften by breathing deeply and imagining herself as a contented kitten.) That's better. I'm not making this into such a big production. Now I'm enjoying how much Jeff seems to care about me, and that definitely turns me on. (Every few minutes her habit of *trying* to feel sexy sneaks back and distracts her. But the more she lets go of trying, the more excited she becomes.)

Pleasure and anxious effort are like two different channels on a TV set. If a person struggles to become aroused or to attain an orgasm, that switches the channel from "enjoyment" to "anxiety." Realistically, we can't always have control over which channel is in operation. Sometimes we have every reason to be mad with passion, but unconsciously we're upset about something. It's humbling to realize that we aren't always the masters of our minds, but neither is any other man or woman on earth. The best thing is to let go of struggling, and remember that quiet little pleasures are also delightful. Enjoy some gentle affection, appreciate the things you like about your partner, do something nice for him or her, or shift to a different activity for a while.

Remember to change demands into preferences. After all, there are far more satisfactions in life than any person can possibly absorb. You might prefer to be in wild sexual abandon, but you don't have to demand it. It's wonderful to lie with your lover, having your face caressed.

Another distracting bedtime attitude involves working hard to be a good lover. If you become preoccupied with "technique," your partner will sense your self-consciousness and experience less pleasure than if you simply enjoyed the intimate moment. What makes a person good in bed is wholehearted *participation*, not just the ability to make all the right moves.

Some people are relaxed about their own lovemaking, but over-regulate their partner. "Here's the right way to rub my back," they may say, "and this is the right way to nibble my earlobe." There's a big difference between asking for what you want and rigidly monitoring a lover's behavior.

We also frustrate ourselves if we become perfectionistic about sex. We may feel jumpy because the phone keeps ringing and we wish we'd left it off the hook. Or maybe our orgasm wasn't strong, or we didn't feel as tender as usual, or we were tired. If we let go of trying to make it better, we'll appreciate how good it really was.

Key Ideas from Chapter Ten

It's surprising how often pleasure intertwines with feelings of unease. Sometimes this is because we're trying to control our pleasure—to increase it, decrease it, or otherwise regulate it—just as we're trying to control everything else in life. The less we overcontrol, the more we'll be free to enjoy.

11

Pressures at Work
The Easy-Effort Solution

Most people's problems center around two main areas—work and relationships. Job pressures are almost universal; work creates stress, and stress in turn interferes with work. Stress-related symptoms such as absenteeism cost businesses between fifty and seventy-five billion dollars per year in the U.S. alone—up to $750 per worker. Fortunately most on-the-job frustrations can be alleviated.

Cutting Job Stress Down to Size

Let's go back to the idea from Chapter Four that many stresses are actually non-problems, pseudo-problems. As you may recall, we can consider something to be a pseudo-problem if it (1) doesn't harm us physically and (2) doesn't upset us much if we maintain a positive attitude.

Saying we upset ourselves at work with non-problems does *not* mean these issues are insignificant, or that they should be ignored, or that we're childish to let them bother us. What it does mean is that we could feel better by adjusting our attitudes, even if the problem stays exactly the same.

The following charts lists (I) job-related pressures, (II) ways people tense themselves up because of these pressures, (III) the resulting emotions, and (IV) negative behaviors that make the situation even worse.

I. Work Problems

Impending deadline	Upcoming review	Incompetent boss	Unexciting work
Criticism	Low salary	Distractions	Exacting work
Mechanical failure	Labor dispute	Ethical issues	Ugly workplace
Misplaced papers or tools	Personality clash	Complicated work	Lack of recognition
Too many tasks	Incompetent subordinate	Unpredictable work	Not close to co-workers

II. In Reacting to Work Problems, People Struggle:

Against disapproval	To understand a co-worker	To be assertive	Against the clock
For approval	To remember things	To control a situation	To improve
To win	For fairness	To change someone	To be somewhere else
To resolve problems	To make decisions		To be understood

III. Resulting Feelings

Anger	Embarrassment	Self-pity	Envy
Fear	Disgust	Depression	Vengefulness
Weariness	Shame	Boredom	Hatred
Sadness	Confusion	Anxiety	Panic
Frustration	Ambivalence	Gloom	Resignation
Guilt	Self-righteousness	Worry	Apathy

IV. Resulting Behaviors and Symptoms

Confusion	Outbursts	Avoidance	Alcohol and drug abuse
Muscle tension	Arguments	Withdrawal	Passive resistance
Headaches	Sarcasm	Absenteeism	Deliberate sabotage
Colitis	Rudeness	Lateness	
Daydreaming	Tiredness	Forgetting things	

Here's an example of how to apply these charts. Len and Maria both disliked their co-worker, Clint, who was a master at blaming other people every time he bollixed up a project. Len's response was to avoid Clint and to wish the work day would be over. He felt frustration and weariness, which resulted in absenteeism. Maria, on the other hand, was feisty. She would get into power struggles (straining for control), and she became habitually sarcastic to Clint. Same issue, but different responses.

Look at Section I in the chart, and find a problem you've tripped over a few times. What forms of straining resulted (Section II)? How did you feel and act (Sections III and IV)? If you let go of some of the tension, how might you feel and act differently? Might part of the frustration turn out to be a non-problem?

To learn more about the difference between real problems and pseudo-problems, let's consider another example. Craig, who travels around the country troubleshooting his company's computers, is a ruddy-faced fellow with blue eyes that seem almost iridescent. He tends to react strongly to customer complaints:

> "I listen to their gripes and I get impatient. When they start a sentence, I know what they're going to say already, but they need to spill it all out and relieve themselves, while I stand there tapping my foot. Sometimes I want to yell at them, 'If you'd just shut up I can tell you how to fix the damned thing in two minutes.'"

So customers are aiming harsh noises and angry looks in Craig's direction. That's a pseudo-problem, because they're criticizing the company, not Craig himself. He's not being threatened in any way. They're also taking up Craig's time. This is a pseudo-problem, because Craig is paid to spend a reasonable portion of his time listening to complaints. It's part of his job. The only real problem is that he needs to restore the client's confidence. Experience has proven that he does that very well, so this actual problem is much smaller than the pseudo-problems of harsh sounds, angry frowns, and "wasted" time.

Compare Craig with Victor, who taught wood and metal shop to high school students. Victor loved teaching, but he hated disciplining malcontents. Unfortunately, shop was used as a "dumping ground." Unruly students who couldn't make it elsewhere were channeled into Victor's classes. Their antics ranged from that of the fellow who made a coffee table with an X-rated scene on the underside to the not-so-amusing bruiser who attacked a classmate with a saw—a dull one, fortunately. Victor clearly had an actual problem: He had to be alert and energetic in maintaining order. This was a real problem, in the sense that even a very positive person would have found it frustrating. But on top of that, Victor had a larger pseudo-problem— his belief that students "shouldn't" need much disciplining, and his judgment that he himself was a failure because he spent so much time keeping youngsters in line.

Remember, referring to these issues as non-problems does not mean they're unimportant. If Victor convinced his superintendent to send him fewer unruly students, obviously he would accomplish more. Perhaps Victor will even decide to change jobs. But here and now, fretting about the situation only *adds another layer to his tensions*.

As we saw in Chapter Four, asking ourselves simple questions can give us new perspective on personal frustrations. Here are some questions that relate to work issues:

- Can I protect my own vital interests? Is there any danger of losing my job, my salary, or the long-term respect of others?
- Is this any worse than what others go through? Don't others have to work late/handle unfair criticism/admit mistakes/make tough decisions/take a risk and wait to see if it pays off?
- Does my self-esteem need to depend on how well I perform this task?
- Does my self-esteem need to depend on what this person thinks of me?
- Can I do my best, and let that be sufficient?

A few helpful affirmations include:

- Every day I learn more about the job, my co-workers, and how I can be more effective.
- I can handle setbacks without exaggerating their importance.
- I can watch out for difficult people, and steer away from needless conflicts.
- I can assert myself without being abrasive.
- This task is dull, but it's not difficult.
- This task is difficult, but it's not dull.

- I learn from every mistake.
- This is like a card game; I can't choose the cards I get, but I can find out how to play them.
- I'll be here all day, so I might as well enjoy it.

Easy Effort

To avoid manufacturing non-problems, we can let go and relax. This doesn't mean we become jellyfish, floating with the tides. Every task takes effort and decisiveness. But there's a big difference between hard effort and easy effort.

Hard effort has its place in life. When a runner in the New York Marathon is grinding out that final mile, the mind and the body are fighting, forcing, and struggling. Strain and tension are absolutely appropriate.

On the other hand, the first twenty-five miles of the race called for easy effort. Effort was involved, as a concentration and channeling of power. But it had to be a calm, relaxed, and clearly focused effort. Any excess tension would drain off the energy that was needed for the final sprint.

Auto-racing legend Bobby Rahal said a few days before winning the 1986 Indianapolis 500, "The key to any race is to really almost psych yourself down." A calmer driver, he suggested, would think more clearly, tire less easily, and be less dominated by emotions.

Few of our projects require a do-or-die dash for the finish. Generally we're running the steadier phase of the race in which energy must be expended, but also conserved. We need to maintain a peaceful and positive outlook, an awareness of the task at hand, and a sensitivity to the way our partners in the game are moving and shifting. Easy *does* it.

Here is a diagram that shows four different combinations of tension levels and activity levels.

1 Attitude: TENSE Behavior: PASSIVE	2 Attitude: RELAXED Behavior: PASSIVE
3 Attitude: TENSE Behavior: ACTIVE	4 Attitude: RELAXED Behavior: ACTIVE

Inner Tension Levels and Outer Activity Levels

In the first pattern, *tense-passive*, the person is exploding inside but ineffectual on the outside. At work, people often strain and worry about a task even before they actually begin. It's like a little boy looking wistfully out the window at the grass he has to cut, wishing he could get it mowed by remote control.

The *relaxed-passive* individual is comfortable, carefree, and unproductive. This is a childlike attitude. It may look like letting go, but letting go is not a decision to work less skillfully or to become lackadaisical. Instead, it reduces the quantity of *inner* work, the quantity of muscular and psychological strain.

Tense-active typifies those who adopt the rat-race urban-suburban lifestyle. These individuals definitely get things done, and they think the way to do so is through straining—tensely trying to force each situation to turn out right. They assume that they're efficient because of being tense, rather than in spite of it.

Relaxed-active combines the best of both. These people intend for their lives to work, but they aren't stuck in a continual crisis of do-or-die. They're motivated, rather than driven, combining high aspirations with low anxiety. Where some people use tension to keep themselves going, relaxed-active people use *intention*. They have zest and staying power, and can accomplish a lot without weariness. Because they're not distracted by needless anxieties, they frequently become fascinated with the tasks at hand. When they're absorbed in a project it seems less like a burden, and more like a puzzle, a meditation, an athletic challenge, or even a game.

Relaxed-active people know that letting go is not the same as giving up. They don't have to *be* lax to *relax*.

Repeating simple affirmations helps people work effectively without burning out. Try using statements such as, "I accomplish what I need, without rushing," "I can be fully relaxed, and fully energized," or *"At this moment, life is effortless."*

That last affirmation is deceptively powerful. It reminds us that at any given moment, very little exertion or "oomph" is needed to handle our tasks. Right now, you're reading a book. There's no need to struggle to read the words or understand the concepts. Understanding comes from reflection, not from locking the jaw, holding the breath, and squeezing muscle fibers in the forehead. We needn't make enormous efforts to carry out the simple activities of life, such as walking, reading, writing, thinking, conversing, exercising, driving, praying, eating, lovemaking, and handling physical objects. Every one of these behaviors can be virtually effortless. In a way, anything that's possible at all is actually easy. (And that's easy for all of us to forget.)

The Stress Factory at Work

Let's look further at the ways our minds manufacture job dissatisfaction, starting with our old friend, "pushing."

Overfocusing is a common form of pushing. People assume that since some concentration is good, more concentration must be better. Actually, each task involves an optimum level of focused attention. Beyond that point, efficiency declines.

————□————

Method 26: The Mental Speedometer

Special benefits: Eliminates the rapid and jumbled thinking that results from pushing ourselves.

Observe your thoughts and assign them an imaginary "speed," such as 150 mph. Then suggest to yourself that they're slowing down to 140 . . . 130 . . . 120, and so on. You may even visualize a speedometer, with the needle slowly dropping, and imagine your foot lifting off of the accelerator pedal. Many people are surprised at how quickly this technique calms them down, especially if they deepen their breathing at the same time.

———————□———————

In addition to pushing, *resistance* is also common at work. When they arrive at work, people put on their resistance like a suit of clothing. It's as if they were wearing a T-shirt that says, "I'd rather be anywhere but here." They wear their resistance uniform all day, and then go home and take it off for a few hours.

Some people use resistance to a job to motivate themselves to look for another one. But spending eight hours a day with a tight gut is a fairly crude method of reminding oneself not to stay at Grouchwell Corporation.

Of course, resistance can also show up at home. One fellow described his reluctance to do housecleaning: "I used to think doing chores 'wasn't life.' It seemed like time out of my allotted lifespan, time that could never be recovered. I needed to hurry and finish so I could start living again."

Resistance makes the smallest tasks into Herculean labors. Think about dental flossing, for example. We know we have to floss our teeth if we want to keep them. Our dentists have made that excruciatingly clear, have they not? But it's awkward, it's uncomfortable, it tastes funny, the floss tears off between the molars, and you have to dig that out with more floss, and there are all those sticky little stains on the mirror. Couldn't we put it off until tomorrow night?

The opposite of resistance is willing participation, injecting ourselves into every activity. By moving toward what we're doing instead of constantly leaning away from it, we can become more comfortable with life as it is.

Having examined pushing and resisting, let's consider a third form of on-the-job pressure, *self-consciousness.*

When we're self-conscious, we're concentrating both on what we're doing and on how it appears to others. It's hard to be effective when the mind is thus divided. While trying to make a sale, for example, people often wonder, "What do they think of me? How does my face look? Should I take my hands out of my pockets? Where should I put them? Am I animated enough? Forceful enough? Funny enough?" All this is most distracting. When we're trying to make an impression, we make an impression of "trying."

To reduce self-consciousness, let go for a few seconds and then firmly refocus on the task at hand. As Gestalt therapist Fritz Perls pointed out, the best antidote to self-consciousness is to become absorbed in what's happening right this minute.

When the End is Nowhere in Sight

At times, our capacity to work is pushed to the limit. For some of us this happened during final exams in college, but even outside college it's not unusual for people to put in fourteen-hour days for weeks or even months. Teachers, for instance, go through periods when they're grading seemingly endless piles of papers. In addition, people who work normal hours may have a physical or emotional handicap that makes a forty-hour week seem like eighty.

In dealing with overwhelming commitments, the best approach is to relax and focus on the present. Let go, using any techniques that work for you. You might try "just for now" (Chapter Six) or changing demands into preferences: "I'd prefer to get to bed before 2:00 a.m., but I don't absolutely have to." Take things one moment at a time. By asking, "What do I need to do *now?*" we can cut each task down to size.

Incidentally, you can maximize your use of the strategies described in this chapter by combining them with the reminder-techniques listed in Chapter Six.

Hurrying can be stimulating for a while, but tearing along in a frenzy for endless hours is inefficient or even physically harmful. Be especially careful to pace yourself after you become good at releasing tensions. Don't press yourself beyond your own physical limitations.

Saving Face

A pleasing appearance is important at work, and a relaxed person's face makes a very different impression than the face of someone who's worried or irritated.

Claire, a 36-year-old executive secretary, made a powerful discovery while applying for a higher-paying job. A few minutes after the last, make-or-break interview, she glimpsed her own face as she passed a mirror. The strain she had been feeling inside was plainly visible in the lines around her eyes and the set of her mouth. Claire didn't get the job, but she did receive a valuable lesson: "Nowadays I make up my face from the outside first, with cosmetics. Then I make it up from the inside, with relaxation."

The face is the most public part of your body. It's always on display and it acts as a virtual magnet for muscular tension. But no one can arrange to sit for a facial every time his or her forehead begins to crease. Fortunately, we can learn to melt off the tension right in the middle of a business luncheon or a high-pressure conference.

A facial self-survey. The first step in learning facial relaxation is to pinpoint your personal tension spots. Let's begin with the forehead. Lots of people hold the skin in their foreheads up or down or pulled in toward the bridge of the nose. I know a fellow who always looks startled, because of the way he elevates his eyebrows. After several decades of doing eyebrow pushups, his brow is permanently creased with deep, wavy lines.

Next, notice the way your eyes feel. Do they seem to be pushing forward, or squeezing themselves tight? Are they steely, as if you were trying to stare down Dirty Harry?

Check your mouth and jaw. Many people unconsciously clench the jaw as if they were hanging by their teeth from a high wire. The center of all this rigidity is a spot just behind your back teeth. Try rubbing the area, and notice any tenderness. This spot may need a lot of gentle massage, which is easy to do at odd moments. As the jaw relaxes, you will see lines of pressure fading, from your forehead to your chin.

Never type with your forehead. Do you scrunch up your face whenever you concentrate on something like typing or reading? One remedy for this habit is to deliberately make the facial muscles slightly tighter, for about 60 seconds. After a moment of exaggerated tension, the muscles rebound into relaxation.

The "no hands" facial. There are ways to give yourself a concentrated facial without adding extra time to your schedule—and without even using your hands. Use the relaxation imagery from Chapter Two while watching TV, listening to music, doing yoga, playing a quiet game with your children, going for a walk, eating a leisurely meal, chatting on the phone, enduring a dull meeting, getting a haircut, or visiting the beauty salon. By releasing facial stresses in the midst of life's bustle and confusion, you can look younger, happier, and more vital—from the inside out.

Key Ideas from Chapter Eleven

Many of us habitually strain and struggle in the workplace. It's better to pace ourselves through the day, substituting easy effort for hard effort. When we encounter a problem, either we can solve it or we cannot. If we can solve it, why strain? If we can't, then struggling and thrashing around inside of our own brains isn't going to get us anywhere either. Easy *does* it.

12

Redesigning Your Own Habits

When I ask people what they want to change about themselves, they usually mention their habits. They want to quit smoking, lose weight, stop procrastinating, and start exercising regularly.

Because habits seem difficult to change, one can find hundreds of books and workshops on reshaping personal behaviors. I won't try to sum up all the tips and formulas that are available. But no matter what plan you follow for diet or exercise or nailbiting control, it will work more smoothly if you remember to relax and let go.

Let's start by thinking about how habits are formed. The key ingredient is repetition. If someone wraps a tiny thread around a circus strong man, he'll obviously have no trouble breaking it. But suppose that this same tiny thread is wrapped around him a hundred thousand times. Now the muscle man has become a prisoner. Repeated actions are like that tiny thread.

After hundreds of repetitions, it's as if a groove has been worn into the mind. The destructive pattern is now the path of least resistance. To change our behavior, we have to keep ourselves out of the old groove and send ourselves down a different pathway. When we notice ourselves sliding into the familiar groove of reaching for the second helping we switch over to the new groove of fixing tea instead. After a while we've deepened the new groove through practice, and the old groove has gathered dust through disuse.

Friction-Proofing Your Own Mind

For at least two reasons, learning to cope with tension makes it easier to shift our behaviors.

1. Easing the stress of change. When we modify our habits, we experience distress. In giving up Valium, there's physical and emotional craving. In controlling our spending, there's a sense of deprivation. In learning to speak up in a meeting, there are sweaty palms and a pounding heart.

While jogging, one runner encountered a weighty, oppressive feeling, as if his body couldn't go on. When he observed how his legs actually felt, they were OK. His "pain" was a pattern of thoughts, attitudes, images, and emotions more than a muscular sensation. Often we have a *belief* that we're hurting, so we dwell on the pain and dramatize its importance: "Poor me!" But when we look closely, the discomfort dissolves like fog in the morning sun.

So our thoughts may tell us we're suffering, even though the actual sensations of unhappiness are fairly mild. As usual, ninety percent of the stress comes from our attitude about a problem, and only a small fraction from the problem itself. The key principle to remember—and it's, oh, so easy to forget—is that *mild discomfort is not a problem.*

Method 27: How Bad Is It?

Special benefits: Helps us become realistic about discomforts.

When you're resisting some chore, or denying yourself a seductive but destructive pleasure, objectively evaluate the uncomfortable sensations. Rate the sensations on this scale, from one to five:

5: Absolute agony.

4: A discomfort that cannot be endured for more than an hour.

3: A feeling that's quite unpleasant, but that can be tolerated to gain something of value.

2: Moderate discomfort.

1: Mild discomfort, like an itch or an ache.

Here's what people often find when they rate their own distress:

- I supposedly "hate" cleaning the kitchen floor, but all I feel as I use the mop is a mild restlessness. It's a "two" on the discomfort scale.
- For three hours I've been doing my homework. But my only discomfort is a tired bottom and some burning in my eyes—it's really a one on the one-to-five scale.

We can handle such situations if we let go, relax, and don't over-dramatize matters. By refusing to magnify mild discomfort, we can conquer destructive habits more rapidly.

Certain affirmations can strengthen our resolve:

- I'll be proud when I finish this project.
- I'm strong enough to handle tough challenges.
- As time goes by, my self-discipline gets better and better.
- I can endure *anything* for half an hour, if it's important to me.
- I won't let habits and impulses run my life.

Additional Tips: Chores are easier with a soundtrack. Put an extension cord on your tape recorder and listen to Mozart while you wax the car. It also helps if you dwell on things you're looking forward to, while you carry out a task.

2. Unlocking the battle between parent and child. Old habits fulfill unconscious needs. When people try to stick to a budget, for instance, the mind usually resists. Sometimes such individuals can visualize a child inside of themselves, who feels deprived and wants more, more, more. It's valuable to bring that personality into consciousness, and find out what's bothering it. Maybe it wants love, for example, and it accepts shiny gadgets as a substitute.

Commonly people are locked into an ongoing conflict between the Critical Parent and the Criticized Child (Chapter Eight). The internal parent says, "You've had enough to drink." The rebellious, greedy child rationalizes: "Just one more and I'll stop." And after one more, the child is that much stronger.

Louie wanted to shed about twenty pounds, but he seldom stuck to a diet. In counseling he investigated the "voices" that spoke when he was tempted to overeat. One set of thoughts sounded like a little boy: "Please let me have the

cookie—just this once!" Another voice scolded him—
"You're such a slob"—but didn't effectively curtail the
overeating pattern. A third voice, a sort of umpire, made
peace between the other two by rationalizing: "A few
cookies now, but no dessert tonight." (Of course he ra-
tionalized again when dessert appeared.) In order for Louie
to change, he could begin to soothe the child-part, showing him that he really wants love, not Oreos. He could tell
the scolding voices to back off, and challenge the "umpire"
to come up with compromises he would actually honor.

Note: Struggle sometimes helps. With particularly powerful patterns, people may go through a "white knuckle" phase, in which
they're hanging on to their resolve by sheer force of will. Some people who quit smoking need to practically handcuff themselves to keep
away from cigarettes. This is one of the few situations in which mental
strain and tension may be the best alternative, at least for a while.

The Seven Stages of Self-Directed Change

We go through several important stages when we alter our own
habits, and it's dangerous to ignore any of them. Those of us in the
helping professions can assist our clients in recognizing these phases.
(The order of the stages may vary, of course, and they often overlap.)

1. Making a commitment. We start by dedicating ourselves to our
goal, so it becomes a top priority. Many people skip this step. They
decide that, "Since I'm now thirty pounds overweight, I have to start
dieting immediately." But it's a terrible mistake to start a diet
prematurely. Struggling becomes a substitute for commitment, and
such halfhearted efforts usually result in discouragement.

If you haven't clearly decided to make a particular change, think
about it for a few days longer. In the meantime you can hold the
line by slightly modifying your behavior. Even if you're not ready
to set a budget, for instance, you can cut down on everyday spending.

Ask yourself, "Do I want to change or do I only think I should?"
If most of your motivation comes from a nagging conscience, it may
not be time to commit. But if you're genuinely tired of following patterns that harm you, then perhaps you're ready.

2. Forming a strategy. Plan your strategy carefully. Take a few days
to observe the habit you'll be altering. What cues set it in motion?
When and where does it operate? What emotions and attitudes keep

it going?

Develop tactics that *modify the behavioral sequence.* If you're trying to quit smoking, for instance, try waiting fifteen minutes after you decide you want a cigarette. You can also put the ashtray behind you so you have to turn around every time you take a puff. Anything that makes the pattern less automated will give you greater control.

3. Beginning. As you apply your strategy, notice whether you're encouraging or discouraging yourself. We often discourage ourselves by assuming that habits should be easy to rearrange. After all, we're only trying to alter the way our minds work. If we were digging a trench or painting the house we'd expect it to be hard, but it shouldn't be such a chore to balance the checkbook . . . should it?

In a way, change is very simple. It consists of *deciding to act differently, remembering to follow through, and tolerating mild discomfort.* But in practice, most of us experience change as difficult. Here are three suggestions that make it easier:

A. Break the process into small increments. If you want to go on a 1200-calorie diet, you might start off with 1800 calories. As you go through the day, notice that the discomfort this causes is tolerable. Then cut down to 1500 calories, and so on.

B. Approach a new habit experimentally. If you've been drinking too much lately, skip a drink and see how you feel later. Put it in the context of your *overall level of happiness.* If you don't take the drink (or buy the sweater, or watch the time-wasting TV show), how do you feel in an hour, or a day? Usually you'll feel fine, which tells you that it's not a big deal.

C. To accentuate the positive, count the number of times that you see improvement. If you're a chart-keeper, you can graph your daily progress.

4. Ambivalence. This stage arrives after you've begun to alter a pattern but before your progress is solid. The mind may start telling you, "This is taking too long; it's too hard." Try letting go *just for now,* as explained in Chapter Six. Since habits are best altered one day at a time, or even one minute at a time, letting go just for now makes the process less of a major production.

5. Overconfidence. Because sticking with the new habit is less of a struggle, we may relax our vigilance and backslide. This phase is almost inevitable, but if we watch for it we can minimize its impact.

Realizing that a temporary relapse doesn't invalidate our progress, we can relax and get back on course.

6. Consolidation. Finally the change in habit begins to sustain itself. A new groove has been worn into the mind and we can slide into that groove instead of into the old pattern. The craving for cigarettes is not as excruciating. There's less resistance to climbing on the exercise bike. We can keep reminding ourselves that *mild discomfort means that we're on the right track.* The battle has shifted in our favor.

7. Victory. This stage may occur after weeks, months or years. At this point the new habit has worn a deeper groove into the mind than the old habit. We now automatically do what's good for us. There are still times when we're tempted, particularly if we are dealing with a physical addiction such as smoking cigarettes. But if we backslide, it's either because of laziness or because of an unhealthy response to stress. And of course, a better way to deal with stress is to use your favorite techniques for letting go.

A Taste for Hunger

Millions of people are concerned with weight control, either because they actually are overweight or because they imagine that it's beautiful to look emaciated. Whatever the reason for dieting, weight control is easier if we learn to tolerate mild discomfort. Hunger is a feeling that people avoid, so a dieter is choosing to have an experience that we label as no-fun. As usual, the mind's criteria as to which experiences are positive and which are negative may have little to do with reality.

Something happened once that showed me how a mild feeling of hunger can seem either pleasant or unpleasant, depending on the way we look at it. In sharing this personal anecdote, I'm not meaning to imply that my experiments with eating or with other habits have always turned out successfully. But this particular experiment was productive, and I learned something. Here's what happened:

A number of years ago I was in the habit of stuffing myself at least twice a day, and my oversized meals acted as a pacifier. They dulled my moods, making me feel less awake, less anxious, and less alert.

I decided that for a month I would eat whatever I wanted, usually in the normal pattern of three meals a day. But I would never eat until I was full.

Occasionally my sensations of hunger were difficult to handle. But frequently the empty feeling in my stomach felt *positive*. For example, one day I ate a light lunch, and about three o'clock I thought I was hungry. I checked my physical sensations, and what I felt was a sort of lightness, a clean and refreshing feeling. My mind had created the concept of "I'm hungry," but it was merely a false alarm.

Around 5:30 I thought once again, "I'm hungry." Yet what I actually felt was a vivid sense of alertness. My mind was noticing that it was dinner time, rather than noticing my own experience, so it told me to seek out food before I needed it. While getting ready for a meeting around 6:30, I heard my mind say, "Now I'm really hungry!" I was worried that I wouldn't be able to eat during the meeting, and I'd be starving by the end of the night.

I went to the meeting and became absorbed in the discussion. I forgot about eating, came back, and went to bed. The next morning I woke up and my mind said "I'm hungry." This time it was right.

Please don't conclude from this story that I'm always the master of my own impulses. But whenever a person catches the mind creating false alarms, it's important to notice and celebrate that experience.

Alcohol and Other Drugs

Drug dependency is a stubborn problem. The stress-release tactics of *Feel Better Now* cannot substitute for professional treatment, but they can certainly help.

> Bill came in for counseling concerned about his drinking. He seldom got drunk, but he was drinking every day as a means of stress control. He began wondering if he had a problem when he was at the grocery checkout with a four-liter wine bottle, and the cashier asked if he was throwing a party. The counselor asked Bill to keep track of exactly how much he drank, and he learned that he was consuming between three and five glasses of wine per day. He found himself thinking, "I'll feel deprived if I don't take a drink." The counselor suggested that if Bill was unable to limit himself to two drinks, he should quit altogether. Bill substituted other beverages for alcohol. When he noticed himself longing for a drink, he used relaxation techniques to let go of the tension.

Many people need to abstain completely, and that requires a lot of letting go. One of the most effective programs is the Twelve Step plan of Alcoholics Anonymous. Can you see how letting go is necessary in these examples of the Twelve Steps?

"We admitted we were powerless over alcohol—that our lives had become unmanageable."

"We made a decision to turn our will and our lives over to the care of God as we understood Him."

"We made a searching and fearless moral inventory of ourselves."

Such steps require letting go of resisting the help of others, bracing against threatening situations, and striving to be right in our own eyes. AA's One Day at a Time approach helps alcoholics let go of trying to control the future, and letting go just for now is a basic tool for getting through each day sober. Finally, AA's *Serenity Prayer* is a powerful antidote to excess struggle and strain:

God grant us the serenity to accept
the things we cannot change,
Courage to change the things we can,
And wisdom to know the difference.

Procrastination

Most procrastinators are discomfort dodgers. They put off things that make them nervous, and therefore feel momentary relief. When they try to go back to the anxiety-producing task, the tension returns and they avoid it again. People who can set their own schedules, such as entrepreneurs, psychotherapists, salespersons, and clergy, are especially tempted to fritter away time in this manner.

Procrastinators need to cultivate *the art of starting*, and this involves dealing with pain. It's a subtle discomfort, not as dramatic as anger or terror, but it can be as irritating as the sound of fingernails on a chalkboard.

Rudy continually put off organizing his reports, sales leads, and other papers at work. When he looked at the mountain of documents, he could feel constriction in his chest. After imagining the tightness softening, like melting candle wax, he began sorting papers with only minor trepidation.

"Worst things first" is a way of using the desire to dodge discomfort to get things done. By starting off with the most unpleasant task, we can look forward to feeling relieved as soon as it's over. Another trick is Albert Ellis' five minute plan, described in his book, *Overcoming Procrastination*. Begin an uncomfortable task and commit yourself to working for only five minutes. After that, you are free to stop. Working for five minutes destroys the illusion that we can't begin. And after we get rolling for five minutes, we can ask ourselves if we'd feel OK about working for five minutes more, and so on.

The techniques of *Feel Better Now* can help us stay on track. Try out the following sequence:

1. Get ready to do what you've been resisting, and use some technique to let go of the uncomfortable feelings that start to come up. Some helpful techniques include Breathing Freely, Undivided Awareness, Body Release, From Demands to Preferences, and the Method of Choice.
2. Begin. (This is important.)
3. Watch every one of the uncomfortable emotions that your mind presents. Let them go, and continue what you've been doing. *Moment by moment*, keep on letting go. When resistance surfaces, use that as an opportunity for learning to release it.

The Power of Positive Addiction

We've mostly been discussing harmful habits, but it's also valuable to build useful habits such as assertiveness, stress reduction, and regular exercise. In many cases these valuable habits result in an instant payoff, and this creates a kind of "positive addiction." One becomes hooked on the happy, expansive feeling that comes from jogging, or the clean-mouth taste after dental flossing. The trick is to stick with the new habit until positive addiction can develop.

To make it easier to establish a new habit, we can practice changing demands into preferences: "I'd prefer not to be panting as I trot around this track, but it's not a big deal." Preferential thinking acts as a lubricant, cutting through the friction that slows so many fine initiatives to a discouraging halt.

Perhaps the most valuable positive habit of all is the habit of changing habits. If self-directed growth becomes an integral part of our lives, we can gently and gradually reshape our thoughts, feelings, and actions. There's no need to restructure twenty different behaviors at once. (In fact, it's too stressful to work with more than three or four at a time.) We gradually become accustomed to stretching our capacities just a little more every week. The gentle pressure that moves us into positive patterns no longer feels like an enemy, or an externally imposed burden. It's simply a part of who we are.

Key Ideas from Chapter Twelve

Releasing our tensions enables us to get through the crucial first stages of self-directed growth. It helps us tolerate the awkward, out of sorts feeling that accompanies new behavior.

It's important to watch the mind as it attempts to nestle back into the old negative groove. Let go, relax, and usually the worst you'll have to deal with is mild discomfort. If you don't resist the discomfort it will be an inconvenience at worst, and a stimulus at best. It's the reassuring signal that you're on the right track, taking charge of your thoughts, feelings, and actions.

13

Atlas at Ease

Most of this book deals with immediate, personal concerns. But you and I are also part of larger systems, systems of politics, economics, giant corporations, and international crises. This larger world challenges us and frustrates us. The result can be overwhelming, as if we were forced into the role of Atlas, carrying the globe on our shoulders.

I personally believe in becoming involved with the larger world, and I'm sure this bias will be obvious in the next few pages. Even so, I won't use this chapter as a soapbox for advocating my own political viewpoint. For example, I like to encourage people to do what they can for world peace. Yet I realize that a conservative will work for peace in one way, a moderate in another way, and a liberal in still another way. I also realize that some readers aren't especially interested in social issues. Even so, the stress management techniques described in this chapter will be useful in any area of life.

Megastresses

People who can courageously confront their own psyches may feel inadequate in dealing with ecology, hunger, or war. Notice whether you feel uneasy about examining these mega-dilemmas, and do a little letting go. It may help to remember that there are a lot of other people working to prop up this old planet. We don't have to carry it all by ourselves.

I am reminded of Melody when I think about this subject. A big, energetic woman with eyes that remind me of sunflowers, Melody is one of those thoughtful individuals who genuinely loves humanity. Yet Melody is totally apolitical.

This issue came up one evening after dinner with some friends in

Bethesda, Maryland. Dane and Carla had been politically active in the seventies, and Dane had lost interest as he got busier at work. "I hate to admit this," he said, "but I don't even vote any more."

"I never watch the news," said Melody. "All those ridiculous wars and bombings make me angry, and I don't see what I can do about any of it."

Carla frowned and put down her coffee. "I often feel that way myself, and yet what happens in another part of the world ends up affecting me. It sounds trite to say it, but we really are all *one*."

"I still believe in democracy," Dane admitted. "I'm proud that people in the U.S. have a lot of influence on their government. But if everybody was as politically apathetic as I am, there wouldn't be any democracy."

"So why won't you get involved?" Carla asked.

He shrugged. "It's easy to procrastinate. If I've got a toothache or a deadline at work, I can't dodge it. World hunger I can dodge, even though I feel guilty. I decided at one point that I needed to get my own life together before I thought about fixing up society. Of course, by the time I have my life together I'll be ninety-nine."

Melody had been sitting with the family cat in her lap. She stopped stroking it and looked up. "What would feel right to me would be working with large problems on a small basis. If I were a Big Sister to someone who doesn't have a mother, I might be doing something about drug abuse."

Melody eventually got involved with a recreation program for inner-city kids. But she still avoids reading the news, and never darkens the doorway of a voting booth. This saddens me, because I think she would cast her vote with intelligence and caring.

Stress reduction techniques can help people like Dane and Melody make the world a better place, without losing their sense of well-being. In fact, inner harmony on the personal level may lead to action on the political level. Sometimes when people stop tensing themselves up about everyday pressures, they become more aware of the bigger picture. Many pioneers in the study of psychology and consciousness are now involved with larger concerns. Carl Rogers, late in life, helped bring politicians together to learn about conflict resolution. Ken Keyes wrote *The Hundredth Monkey*, a valuable essay on nuclear weapons. So some individuals who develop insight into themselves eventually broaden this concern to include social issues.

On the other hand, some people think the total solution to world problems is a relaxed, harmonious mind. If we let go of worrying about the world, they argue, it will automatically get better. Supposedly, relaxation and acceptance have magical effects on people and physical objects. One workshop leader claimed that if your neighbors are playing loud music, you should release your feeling of discomfort and they will turn it down spontaneously. Another seminar leader told about the theft of his new Porsche. Shortly after he accepted the loss as final, the police found his automobile.

When the fellow accepted the loss of his Porsche and instantly got it back, it would be nice to assume that his acceptance caused the car's recovery, and extrapolate that to every situation. Letting go of distress would serve as a magical incantation. Whenever the incantation didn't work, we would assume that the person didn't let go enough. But life seems to turn out best when people combine mental relaxation with positive action.

People also use the idea that the world is in the hands of God to rationalize political passivity. "I don't need to deal with these big issues; everything will turn out as it's meant to be." This is nothing like the message contained in the Old and New Testaments or the Koran. These scriptures say that we have personal responsibility for making life better here on earth.

Based on quasi-religious attitudes, one well-respected speaker proclaimed that he was unafraid of nuclear war. He assured us that we could rely on people with advanced psycho-spiritual powers to take care of us. "If thousands of ICBM's start flying across the North Pole, a few of these folks are going to say *'This shall not be,'* and the energy from one of their fingertips will block those missiles. That's why I don't worry about nuclear war." The two hundred well-dressed and apparently well-educated men and women in attendance broke into happy applause.

Ironically, the lecturer who spoke of zapping missiles with psychic power warned his audience that esoteric mental gymnastics will not guarantee success in business. He kept telling people to make a plan and work it.

Fortunately, most religious leaders are far more practical about planetary concerns. Ministers, priests, and rabbis are unlikely to rely on some Zen master in a monastery to do incidental duty as an anti-ballistic missile device. But many people do use religion and the belief in parapsychological powers as a basis for ignoring world problems. This is true of liberals, conservatives, and moderates alike.

In daily life, even the most vigorous proponents of mind-power combine positive attitudes with practical action. If the garbage sack in the kitchen is full, they don't expect thought waves to make it grow legs and trundle out the back door. Cleaning up the planet is like cleaning the house—it takes a positive attitude *and* there's a lot of garbage to be carried out.

Let's see how letting go, plus positive action, can help us take out the macro-maxi-mega garbage that has piled up on our global doorstep.

Easing In

Because social problems are so vast and complex, we need ways of making it easier to deal with them. Here are some ideas about building a better world without taking on an overwhelming burden.

1. Educating ourselves. Because we can't become an expert on every subject, it's useful to specialize. Select one cause that you care a lot about, and look for relevant books, articles, and television programs.

As we educate ourselves, we may sometimes become upset. In studying hunger, for instance, we may encounter depressing stories and statistics. By watching our own emotional barometers, we can sense when the problem is starting to seem unbearable. Then we can breathe slowly and deeply, and let go of the inner pressure. Remember, there's a difference between wishing things were perfect right this second, and working for things to get better, day by day.

2. Finding our own style and strategy. Many people forget to analyze what they want to do and how they want to do it. They just plunge in and imitate what others have done in the past. Think about questions such as, "Should I concentrate on the causes of a problem or the symptoms?" If you're fighting drug abuse, for example, you may wonder whether low-cost daycare centers could prevent the neglect that sometimes contributes to chemical dependency.

Another question would be, "How much should I support confrontational tactics, such as boycotts and civil disobedience, and how much should I use low-key measures such as lobbying or public education?" (Even in confrontation, it may be wise to avoid extreme hostility. If we show intense anger, the people we're trying to change may sense our tension and respond by pushing back.)

Social activists sometimes take nonviolence training to develop more positive attitudes. One man who teaches people to protest with a peaceful spirit is a Buddhist monk, Thich Nhat Hanh. He suggests that when you start feeling irritated you can immediately half-smile, and then inhale and exhale quietly for three full breaths. Obviously this is a way of letting go.

3. *Participating in organizations.* The shared concern of other men and women makes a social issue seem real, when otherwise it may seem to exist mostly on television. So we need companions on our journey, but taking part in a group often triggers tensions. Perhaps one or two group members have an unpleasant manner, and we begin wishing they were different. If we let go of resenting their idiosyncrasies, we'll see that most of our compatriots are perfectly OK.

After we've taken part for a while, we'll want to affect decisions and actions. If we start struggling for control, the others may sense our pushiness and start resisting us. If we relax and concentrate on *being effective*, the whole organization should benefit.

4. *Avoiding burnout.* If you become a dedicated volunteer, beware of exhausting yourself. An article called "Shedding Light on Burnout" (Cathy Cevoli, *Nuclear Times*, January/February, 1986) notes that it's easy to become discouraged while working on a project where progress is only measurable over a period of years. The article suggests that people set up penultimate goals—short-term goals that further their long-term objectives.

Since it's easy to become disheartened about social issues, we can encourage ourselves with positive ideas:

- Because of people who cared, we've made great progress. (Examples: public education; the emancipation of slaves; mental health reform; and the rights of women, racial minorities, and the handicapped.)
- I benefit from the work of past generations, and today's children will benefit from my work.
- We're all in this together; I will do my part.
- Action gives me a sense of dignity and participation.
- We never know what we can accomplish till we sincerely try.
- Nobody can do everything, but everybody can do something.

5. *Forgiving our adversaries.* Because social problems are handled through the political process, our own program may be opposed by another faction. It's easy to start:

- Straining to overcome our opponents.
- Straining for them to see things as we do.
- Straining to understand how they can be so stupid.

Feelings of hatred hurt us far more than they harm our "enemies." It's best to release our bitterness, and fight the good fight anyway.

Security and Survival

To apply some of these ideas more specifically, let's consider the problem of nuclear weapons. The superpowers have stockpiled thousands of these bombs, many of them mounted on rockets that can span the globe in less than thirty minutes. Whether we are conservatives, liberals, radicals, or moderates, the presence of enough nuclear weapons to destroy civilization is frightening. We have made progress in reducing the threat of war, but that doesn't mean we should become complacent.

Notice how you're feeling as you read these words. If you're aware of physical tension or emotional distress, don't forget to do some letting go.

It isn't necessary to abandon your *concern* about war or your *intention* to make the world a safer place. You're only releasing the frightened *feeling*. It's as if you suddenly confronted a charging bull. That's a big problem, but if the feeling about the bull immobilizes you, you've got two problems—the bull's momentum and your own paralysis. If you reduce the fear, you're back to one problem, and you're freer to jump aside.

One important part of working for a safer world is to communicate with friends, family, and co-workers. You can find suggestions for talking about peace in Joanna Rogers Macy's excellent book, *Despair and Personal Power in the Nuclear Age*. The toughest challenge, of course, involves relating with someone who disagrees with you. I've led workshops on communication between "hawks" and "doves," using role-playing as a training device. We find that whenever disagreement arises, people start trying to control each other. Watch for these signs of tension:

- In yourself: Holding your breath; tightness in your jaw, neck, shoulders, and back; butterflies or burning sensations in your stomach; and a feeling of frustration, exasperation, or self-righteousness.
- In your friend: Facial tension, such as a frown or

grimace; a louder voice; put downs or name calling; and a rigid or aggressive body position, such as crossing the arms or leaning forward as if to invade your territory.

When one of you starts to tense up, let go of pushing and/or resisting your partner. It may help to say, "I don't want to force ideas down your throat," or "I know that we want both peace *and* security for our country, even though we may disagree about how to achieve it." See if you can be open to what your friend is saying. The disagreement can become a chasm to be bridged, rather than a contest to be won or lost.

As I said earlier, emotional harmony is not enough to eliminate world problems. But even though such harmony is not *sufficient* for peace, it's certainly *necessary*. Letting go is one of the foundation stones of a truly peaceful world.

Your Vision of Life

People who work for a better world often base their actions on a deeply felt personal philosophy. Let's examine the way such a philosophy can help us release tensions.

Certain views of the world are especially effective at encouraging serenity. Within the Judeo-Christian tradition, many churches and synagogues teach people to trust: "God loves you and cares for you," they say. To feel supported by a great divine hand is certainly reassuring. One turns life's problems over to God, after doing one's best to resolve them.

Another route to a deep sense of trust is found in Oriental religions such as Zen Buddhism. Zen places more emphasis on meditation than on communion with a divine being. When the mind is quiet, excess effort falls away. Zen can also be combined with other religions. Many Roman Catholics, for example, have explored its disciplines.

Still another pathway is that of humanism, which emphasizes this present life rather than the world beyond. Humanists seek inspiration in nature, in ideas, and in community with other persons. They constitute part of the membership of the Unitarian Universalist Association, Ethical Culture, and Reform Judaism.

Truly, all of these roads can lead to inner peace. To connect with something greater than our own small selves helps us live our lives in trust instead of in anxious trepidation.

———————◻———————

Method 28: Spiritual Reconnection

Special benefits: Integrates religious and philosophical beliefs into everyday living.

When you want to feel better, take a moment to reconnect with something larger than yourself.

- Jews might call to mind a phrase from the Torah, or a Hebrew prayer.
- Protestants might visualize Jesus, or remember the tune of a favorite hymn.
- Roman Catholics might picture the image of Mary, Jesus, or one of the saints.
- Humanists might recall an image that helps them feel a part of nature and the human family.

(These are merely illustrations, of course. Many other examples could have been given.)

———————◻———————

To employ spiritual reconnection as a technique does run the risk of using spirituality for trivial purposes. We are not trying to turn religion into a stress-reduction pill. Instead, we are putting our personal problems in perspective by focusing on what is truly significant.

Key Ideas from Chapter Thirteen

It takes courage to wrestle with political and economic forces. They're so big, and we're so small. But learning to cope with tensions helps us join with others, so that our combined efforts can lift the burden of Atlas.

14

The Recovery of Love

As we have seen, a lot of useless distress results from *tensely try-ing to make every situation turn out right*. This pattern is especially destructive to intimate relationships. Conflicts between intimate part-ners may completely overshadow the love and caring that was once so satisfying. By learning to ease interpersonal tensions, we can often recover these loving feelings. In examining ways to do this we will emphasize communication between husband and wife, but the same principles apply to relationships with friends, relatives, and co-workers.

Forming a Relationship

Taking first things first, we all know that *finding* a mate can be stressful. In getting to know a potential lover, most of us tend to become self-conscious and try too hard. When you're getting ac-quainted with someone attractive, remember that you do not need *this* person. You only need *one* partner, and if it's not this one it will be another. Furthermore, the right person will appreciate you just the way you are. There's no need to make a dazzling impression.

Once you've succeeded in beginning a relationship, other forms of tension may appear. You may find yourself pushing to make the relationship into something it isn't. Most of us have an ideal picture of a spouse or lover. Since no one conforms to that ideal, we try to twist reality into the shape of our fantasies. I've spoken to divorced people who knew even before they were married that it wouldn't work out. They didn't listen to their own better judgment.

It's OK to let go of suppressing our doubts. Even if we're delighted with a relationship, our feelings about a partner are not consistent. No matter how we strain, we cannot process our responses into a smooth, textureless puree. Let the inconsistency be there. Moderate dissatisfactions needn't torpedo a romance.

Letting Yourself Be Close

Once people become romantically linked, they face the thrilling and intimidating challenge of intimacy. In many cases, people are afraid of being engulfed or abandoned by an intimate partner. Those who fear being engulfed may have had dominating or overprotective parents. They brace against intimacy, holding their partners at arm's length. Those who fear abandonment may have had parents who were rejecting or frequently absent. They anxiously cling to their partners. And many people anticipate both engulfment and abandonment: "Don't enjoy me too much, or you'll smother me. Don't enjoy me too little because then you might leave. If you're a bit chilly, I imagine it's the beginning of the end."

One destructive reaction to these fears is to ricochet back and forth between closeness and distance. Lovers may indulge in a sort of interpersonal bulimia, gorging on romantic tenderness and then purging themselves by backing off.

> Frieda and Bert repeatedly battled over trivial disputes, such as "Whose turn is it to change the kitty litter?" These episodes usually followed a good time, as if they had to cancel out the happy experience by bickering.

This couple learned greater flexibility about emotional distance. They began to accept the affection that flowed between them, and they also reduced their need to rush over and nearly drown in each other. Bert in particular was uncomfortable with too much touching, which he referred to as "smoochy kissy-face." He cured himself of this hesitancy through repeated experiences of safe, comfortable skin-to-skin contact with Frieda. Lots of non-demanding tactile pleasuring would eventually charm the quills off a porcupine.

These days, people are frequently getting married or cohabiting after years of living singly. They soon find themselves thinking: "It's jarring to find things out of place in my kitchen." "One of us forgets to do something, and that fouls up the other's plans." "There's a different rhythm; my smooth, efficient system is all mixed up." "We need two bathrooms!"

Letting go is tailor-made for learning to flex, flow, bend, and blend. It helps people cope with:

- Feeling crowded.
- A new daily routine.
- Miscommunications.
- Making compromises.

Some long-time singles have gotten very particular, and may need to work on changing demands into preferences. When there's a conflict with your partner, ask yourself, "Can I accept a range of alternatives, or am I insisting on my way?" Do you have to go to one specific restaurant, or would several others be OK? Could you even go to a movie, snack on popcorn, and eat out some other evening? If you'd resent anything but your favorite options, beware of pernicious pickiness.

How much should a person bend to accommodate a mate? One guideline suggests doing sixty to seventy percent of the giving and allowing the other person to give thirty or forty percent. Because we're more conscious of what we're giving than we are of our partner's sacrifices, what feels like seventy percent is probably more like fifty. (Of course, some agreements can be evaluated objectively, such as a simple financial compromise.) So one formula for a successful relationship is for each party to demand less and give more.

Resistance

> Conrad works long hours at his dry cleaning business, and his wife Beth becomes lonely. She urges him to be home more often. Conrad thinks his independence is at stake and stays away even more frequently, which results in an escalation of demands from his wife.

You can see that by resisting his wife's pressure, the husband winds up with more pressure. Or, in the words of Werner Erhard's famous paradox, "What you resist persists."

Most of the time we get more of what we are stubbornly resisting, and this is true for at least six reasons.

1. Resisting generates tension, tension muddles our thinking, and muddled thinking makes it harder to find the best solution. Have you ever gotten tongue-tied during a confrontation? Later on when you were more relaxed, the right words may have seemed obvious. Stress blocked the flow of communication that might have relieved the original cause of the tension.

2. Resisting often involves repression. Repression involves ignoring reality, and you may need to face certain harsh realities before you find a way to deal with them. If a man ignores his wife's complaints about his sarcasm, he'll keep being sarcastic, and her complaints will persist.

3. Sometimes we tense up, and then get tense about being tense. But by resisting tension, we wind up generating more of it. This is true when we resist a headache, a bout of insomnia, or a feeling of awkwardness while trying to make a good impression. Resisting these forms of tension only makes them worse.

4. It has also been said that we become what we resist. If we fight against something long enough (shyness, for instance), it becomes an important part of our consciousness. We have to watch it carefully in order to fight it, and as a result it fills up our minds. This is why children may end up copying the behavior of their parents even though they swore they wouldn't. Then they pass the same pattern along to their children.

5. Some forms of resistance result in focusing our attention on what's bothering us. If a barking dog is keeping us awake, we may become acutely conscious of the sound. If we let go of fighting the sound, it will gradually fade into the distance. But as long as we are resisting Rover's midnight oratorio, we will "get" more of it. Dwelling upon a problem also stretches out the length of time it seems to last. If one hates a job, the workday goes on forever.

Most of us have experienced the paradox that when we let go of fighting an unpleasant sound it ceases to bother us. I know a fellow who lives near a major airport; his house trembles whenever a plane flies over. In a seminar on letting go, he found that if he stopped bracing against the noise, it didn't seem as loud. This provides an apt metaphor for nearly every frustration we encounter. We can think of a rainy day, a tense relationship, a headache, or a painful emotion as psychic noise. Some of these noises can be turned off, and others can't. But almost all of them will quiet down if we choose to let go.

When something's bothering you, remind yourself that it's only a barking dog. See what happens if you let the dog bark.

6. Resistance generates opposition. This is the paradox of every power struggle: By resisting someone, you give your opponent plenty of exercise in overcoming your resistance. When someone starts an argument, what happens if you argue back? Before long a cycle of push-and-resist has developed, a cycle that takes on a life of its own. It's amazing to see this occur at committee meetings. Everyone wants to have the last word in a controversy, and this keeps the whole dreary discussion trudging along toward nowhere.

One reason we underestimate the destructiveness of inner resistance is that we don't think it shows. "I never speak harshly to Beth, but she's always griping at me," Conrad asserted. If this brilliant but insensitive fellow could see his own icy expression, he'd realize that he's attacking Beth as much as she's provoking him. The difference is that she's up front about it, and he's running a covert operation.

When we resist a friend or an intimate partner, we are probably locking in the behavior we dislike. This is also true in power struggles between teachers and students or employers and employees. We suffer from the delusion that pushing against someone else's behavior will diminish that behavior.

You may recall Aesop's fable about the time the sun and the wind tried to get a man to take off his coat. The wind attempted to blow it off, so the fellow pulled his coat tightly around him. Then the sun came out: "You want to be warm? I'll make you warm as toast." And off came the coat. People will change more readily if we join their desires and interests, rather than contradicting them.

When you don't like somebody's behavior, this behavior is the enemy, not the other person. Do not cooperate with the enemy by resisting it. Do your best to change the disturbing behavior, but stay relaxed inside. Letting go is the surest way to win, and to win without dominating or manipulating.

People hesitate to give up pushing and resisting because it's the only thing they know. Nagging Janie to put away her clothes hasn't worked for five years, but her parents persevere because, "We have to do something." What works better is open communication, genuine listening, consistent rewards and punishments, and lots of positive reinforcement for improvement. In some cases merely abandoning the pattern of push-and-resist will be enough.

> Kelli came into counseling because her husband was astonishingly tyrannical about money. She "knew" he'd never change, but she didn't want a divorce. Instead she wanted to learn to accept him, so she could stay in the marriage. Gradually she began to let go of her resentments. Then one day, for no apparent reason, he asked her how

much money she needed that month and gave it to her without quibbling. She had stopped pushing to make him different, and he had spontaneously changed.

The moral to this story is not that a wife should be long-suffering and hope that her husband will relent. Acceptance cannot replace assertive communication. But if we can take the tug-of-war feeling out of a dispute, the results are sometimes remarkable.

Method 29: Nonresistance

Special benefits: Uses the power of the imagination to protect us from stress.

When a person or a situation is bothering you, think of it as being unpleasant "energy." This negative energy is assaulting your senses much as a loud noise assaults the ear. Then visualize yourself becoming invulnerable: Picture a shield that makes the hurtful energy bounce off, or imagine that it misses you or passes through you harmlessly, as cosmic rays pass through our bodies. If you're being criticized, let the words fly over your head without bothering you.

You don't need to resist or push away something unpleasant. You can simply allow it to be there, without touching you. This technique is especially good in helping people relax about the little quirks of friends and co-workers—nervous habits, coughing, gum-cracking, or irritating tones of voice. If your imagination is good, it can also help you cope with chronic pain or the symptoms of an illness. Here are some affirmations that strengthen this technique:

- I can ignore what's bothering me, and focus on what's useful or enjoyable.
- Negative sensations can't run my life. (Be specific: "This headache can't dictate my mood." "His depression can't pull me down into misery.")

- I can separate myself from other people's emotions.

Disapproval: Showdown at the Not-OK Corral

In many marriages, the husband and wife think that love has completely vanished, when actually it's still there—covered up by anger and frustration. I recall a client who deeply resented his wife and was contemplating divorce. Then his wife was called in for a biopsy, and they found she had breast cancer. I talked with the husband in an empty section of the hospital cafeteria, and at one point he carried out an imaginary dialogue with his wife. We represented her with a salt shaker. As he sat there talking to the salt shaker he recovered tender feelings that had been dormant for years. He was astonished at how much he still loved her, underneath all the resentment.

Resentments in a relationship often boil down to the fact that we disapprove of the other person, and the other person disapproves of us. When we're the disapproving party, we may completely blame the other person for upsetting us. If we're listening to an unpleasant voice, for example, we may assume that the voice causes us to be irritated. But look inside, and see if you're keeping yourself on edge, wishing the voice would go away. You may discover that most of your irritation results from your own tension, from bracing against an unpleasant sound.

Disapproval is the great exaggerator. A raspy voice pricks at our ears, and by tensing up against that tiny discomfort we make it seem like fingernails on a chalkboard. If we stop resisting another individual's personality characteristics, our disapproval will usually diminish.

Here are some things we criticize in other people:

Clothing	Tone of voice
Grooming	Habits of speech
Height	What he/she says
Weight	What he/she does
Race	What he/she doesn't do
Attractiveness	Special problems or vices
Posture	Morals
Facial expression	Intelligence
Gestures	Level of competence
Age	People he/she resembles

In analyzing what you don't like about someone, be as specific as possible. You may discover items such as:

- Her timid driving, upon entering a freeway.
- The way he salts his food before tasting it.
- Her abrupt manner when she answers the phone.
- His habit of losing important papers.

To practice letting go of disapproval, bring to mind some person whom you find mildly frustrating. Turn back to the list of things that we criticize in other people, and see which items apply. Notice any emotions that rise to the surface. These feelings are the primary problem. The person is not stealing food directly out of your mouth or coming after you with a bazooka. The main thing that's happening is that emotions are being stimulated.

See if you can tune into a sense of strain, struggle, or effort. It might involve:

- Wishing the individual were different.
- Struggling to figure out how to change the person.
- Straining to understand the person's actions: "How can he/she be so thoughtless?" (Often we know perfectly well why someone's being cantankerous, but we keep asking "why" anyway.)
- Trying to figure out if he/she is going to bother you in the future.
- Wishing he/she had been different in the past.
- Straining to stop disliking him or her: "Why do I let this person get to me? Why am I so petty?"
- Straining for the person's approval—even if you don't respect your antagonist's judgment.

The tension you feel about this person drains energy, and it probably isn't getting you anywhere. Ask yourself, "Is this tension good for me or bad for me?" See if you would be willing to let go of trying to change him or her, in the past . . . in the present . . . and in the future. Relax, and know that you will do your best, and that this is absolutely all you can do.

You can put another person's idiosyncrasies into perspective by realizing what the two of you have in common.

---□---

Method 30: That's Me

Special benefits: Demonstrates our kinship with other people; helps us drop self-righteousness and develop humility.

As you're observing another person, notice areas in which you're alike. Do this during low-key tasks such as eating dinner, going to a movie, or watching the person talking to someone else. Be aware of both positive and negative traits. Examples of negative traits:

- "Jim forgot our anniversary. Sometimes I neglect things that are equally important to him."
- "Ann's a grouch just before her period—but I'm hard to live with the first hour of every day!"

---□---

Later on when the person does something you dislike, remind yourself that you do similar things. Everybody has faults, but we're still OK. The point of this technique is *not* to excuse bad behavior, but to help ourselves relax and feel better. Reminding ourselves that someone else's faults are fairly ordinary is a rapid and direct way of releasing resentment. In many cases this makes it easier to ask the other person to act differently.

Now let's look at what happens when the shoe is on the other foot.

When people criticize us. Being criticized triggers several forms of tension:

- Wanting to have our own approval. We sometimes lose our own approval when people criticize us, even when the criticism is ridiculous.
- Trying to decide whether the other person's attitude is justified.
- Suppressing our resentment about being criticized.

In love relationships, acceptance and rejection intermingle. A person may enjoy you as a friend, a sexual partner, and a social companion. Yet he or she may have a hard time with some of your moods, or perhaps you resemble a parent or a sibling. You may also represent something that agitates your partner—intimacy, commitment, or the loss of freedom. So you will probably get some mixed messages. If you try to figure out whether your mate Truly Accepts You, you're attempting to solve an impossible riddle. Since trying to do the impossible makes us tense, it's better to ask questions that have answers, such as: "Is this person likely to stay with me in the foreseeable future?"

The weekend visitation. Here is a partly-fictional story that shows how people who are critical of each other can learn to handle their emotions.

Daniel is going to his ex-wife's to pick up his son for a visit. As he turns his car onto her street, he notices that he's holding his breath, and that his shoulders are tense.

Daniel is familiar with some ways of resolving tension quickly, especially the Method of Choice (Chapter Five). Immediately, he tunes into the feeling of straining for control. He discovers that he's straining to know whether she will be in a bad mood. He lets go of trying to predict the future. He notices, and releases, a tension about "not knowing what to say to her." As he parks his car he lets go of "wishing this wasn't such a hassle." His shoulders are more relaxed, now, as he goes up the walkway.

His former wife, Clair, seems stiff and chilly as she opens the door. "Just as cranky as ever," he thinks. He lets go of wishing she were different, and feels calm again. It's as if Clair's chilliness has only to do with Clair, rather than impinging on Daniel's territory. As they talk, she seems less prickly. He relaxes, and feels warmly toward her. With the warm feeling comes "wishing it had worked out between us," accompanied by sadness. He releases the struggle to reconstitute the past. The sadness diminishes.

His son greets him, and they leave together. Clair includes both of them as she wishes them a good weekend. Daniel smiles, wondering if she was being friendly because he was relaxed, or if his relaxation permitted him to see her friendliness. No matter—it feels just fine.

Generally, *the problem is not the situation*, so much as the way we respond to the situation. As Daniel was driving up, nothing was wrong, but he was worrying about the future. There was no actual problem; he was just driving down the street. When Clair greeted him his mind exaggerated her coolness and created an upset by judging that she should be different. After easing these tensions, he noticed that she wasn't being unfriendly. And even if Clair had been hostile, letting go would have helped protect him from her negative attitude.

Straining for control doesn't make us effective. Notice that most of the time, Daniel was straining for things he couldn't have: the power to control the future, to control Clair's attitudes, and to reorder the past. *Whether we can or cannot resolve a problem, we're better off letting go.*

Saying Good-bye

Breaking up is one of the most difficult kinds of letting go. It's tragic to see how many people are still depressed and bitter, ten or fifteen years after a divorce. They need to let go of anger, guilt, sadness, and self-pity.

One especially useless form of self-torture involves asking "why?" It's no doubt valuable to understand why a relationship capsized, so as to prevent a similar loss in the future. But people go on asking why forever, even though they either know the answer or don't know it and never will. Often this sort of rumination is a way of trying to change the past, pushing the pieces of the puzzle around in the hope that they'll finally fit.

Splitting up can be devastating because the part of us that feels abandoned after a separation is the inner child. We look to an intimate partner to nurture us in the same way our parents did—or in the way we wanted them to. When the nurturing becomes unavailable, we feel rejected. And the feeling of abandonment is often present even in the party who left. As a client explained, "My inner adult left Kathy, but my inner child feels like she went away."

Here's how one woman used letting go to help cope with a breakup. Ramona, age forty-five, has been divorced for six years. Recently she went for nearly a year with Joey, and he broke it off after becoming involved with someone else.

It's Saturday night, and although she wants to go visit friends, Ramona is sitting in her apartment staring at the goldfish. She knows some strategies for handling depression, and here are the thoughts that pass through her mind:

"I'd like to be free of this sad feeling that's fogging me in tonight. It's probably a good idea to use some sort of technique, because this is a tough mood to shake. I'll try imagining the child part of me, and see what she's doing." (Ramona has explored her inner child before, and knows that this part of her is vulnerable and a bit melodramatic. She calls her the Little Waif.)

"I can see the Little Waif looking at the door, reaching out her arms, asking for Joey. She's frozen there, hoping he'll come, but he isn't coming. I can feel tears, and I'm holding my breath. (She allows her breath to soften.) I can see how the Waif is straining—struggling for him to come back, struggling for him to be here, struggling for him never to have left.

"I'll exaggerate the way she's struggling by seeing her down on her knees reaching toward the door. Now she's yelling at him, making rude faces and nasty gestures—I like that anger! (She stays angry for a while.) Now it's tiring to be mad, as if by being mad I'm still straining for his love. Let's imagine the Waif giving herself some TLC. (She rubs her own neck for five minutes.) This fantasy hasn't made me feel like everything's roses and honey, but at least I can *move* again. Now that I don't feel stuck in the mud, I'm picking up my coat and heading for the door."

People like Ramona, who have lost a loved one through separation or death, will naturally feel painful emotions for a long while. Many psychotherapists agree that those who suppress emotion after such an experience may carry their hurts inside for years. The memory is like a time-release capsule of poison, walled off from awareness. Even so, there's no reason to spin for months in a whirlpool of grief. You can use the techniques of *Feel Better Now* to give yourself a respite from heartache.

When the Child Rebels

When we think of rebelliousness, we think of teenagers. As our sons and daughters grow up, parental rules and regulations become a challenge to their autonomy. Therefore getting upset about the way your youngster leaves candy wrappers around the house may end up increasing that very behavior. Often some specific issue becomes a symbolic test of power. If the child is four, it might be about eating broccoli. With a sixteen year old the Big Issue may be the latest report card. When people stop inwardly pushing to make the problem turn out right, it becomes easier to resolve.

Despite the reputation they've developed, teenagers have no monopoly on negativism. A fifty year old, for instance, may still be stuck in a rebellious-child syndrome at work, with the boss representing his mean old mama. Although he consciously tries to do better, he still keeps acting like a brat.

Another example would be the husband who wants his wife to stop holing up in the house all day. He tries to shame her into taking some classes: "Judy Schwartz is almost ready to get her degree. If you'd begun five years ago when she did, you'd be finished. Why can't you get off your behind?"

Sometimes a verbal kick in the posterior is effective, but often it makes the other person feel defensive. This reinforces helplessness and discourages confident action.

In dealing with a negativistic individual, let go of tying your own happiness to whether the other person "sees the light." You will feel less desperate, and you'll be more likely to get the outcome you want.

We've seen how releasing tension helps us soften rigid power struggles and minimize feelings of disapproval. It can also help us assert ourselves.

Assertion without Exhaustion

Have you learned the difference between passivity, aggression, and assertion? Too many people flip-flop between passivity (being nice, not rocking the boat) and aggression (attacking, name-calling, or retaliation). Assertion is a more effective approach. It involves saying what we want, clearly and without manipulation.

Assertiveness and releasing tension belong together. Assertiveness without letting go can lead to tense, prickly, covertly aggressive behavior. But letting go without assertiveness might become wishy-washy.

If you want to become more assertive, write down statements such as the following and carry them in your wallet or purse:

- I'm as important as other people. I have legitimate wants and needs.
- If I don't take care of myself, I won't be of much help to others.
- Others ask for what they want, and so can I.
- If I don't stand up for myself, who will?
- Being assertive sets a good example for my children.
- Everybody needs to say "no" sometimes.

Identifying your feelings is a key to assertive living. It's hard to decide what to ask for, or when to say "no," if you aren't in touch with your emotions. The I feel/I want exercise (Chapter Nine) is helpful, and so is the emotional barometer approach (Chapter One). Here's an example:

Penny and her boyfriend were setting up house, and it was taking weeks to get organized. Penny felt especially depressed about the perpetual mess on the kitchen table.

"I tried saying out loud the things that I *felt* and the things that I *wanted* as I looked at the junk on the table," Penny said. "It seemed silly to use this exercise on such a minor irritation, but the minor irritation was bothering me in a major way. Suddenly I found myself saying, 'I don't want him to leave.' I realized that as things were falling apart in my previous marriage, there was constantly a mess on the kitchen table! So back then, mess-on-table meant relationship was ending. But today, mess-on-table means setting up new home. Same mess—different message!"

Penny was able to relax about the table after realizing why she'd been upset. On the other hand, when Penny tuned into her feelings about her boyfriend's evening job, her concern increased rather than decreased. She saw that the longer their schedules kept them away from each other, the more distant they became. He agreed, and in two months was able to arrange a more compatible routine.

For the last few chapters we've been applying the ideas of *Feel Better Now* to job stress, pleasure-anxieties, changing habits, political issues, and conflicts in relationships. You may want to select one or two of these areas for special attention. Which ideas or techniques would help you the most with these concerns?

Key Ideas from Chapter Fourteen

Many close relationships include locked-in patterns of struggle. Each person wants to control the other and resist being controlled, change the other and resist being changed. But grasping for control usually boomerangs. When we push for something we often can't have it, and when we resist something we get lots of it. If we stop pressuring people they may relax, drop their defensiveness, and begin to listen. At that point we can recover loving feelings that have long been dormant, and everybody wins.

15

Dancing with Your Mind

"I don't give a fig for the simplicity on this side of complexity. But I would give my life for the simplicity on the other side of complexity."
— Oliver Wendell Holmes

As Holmes realized, a wise person sees the *simplicity behind the complexity behind the simplicity*. If we only touch the surface of life, it all seems simple. When we look more closely, we find a bewildering hodgepodge of problems, pressures, questions, and alternatives. Eventually we discover certain basic patterns that appear in every tangled predicament. Understanding these patterns helps us relieve stresses and slip through apparent impasses. So now that we've reached the final chapter, let's summarize a few simple ideas that can help us with many perplexing challenges.

Change the Jitterbug into a Waltz

Whenever we feel bad, there's a temptation to fight with our feelings, to kick out the painful emotions as quickly as possible. But it's better to dance with the mind than to fight with it.

Many of the methods in *Feel Better Now* are a lot like dancing with the mind. We start the dance by following, and end up by leading. At first, we carefully follow our own thoughts and feelings. We tune into our tense muscles, we listen to our emotions, we recognize our rigid expectations, we experience the pushing, bracing, and dithering. Then after following our feelings, we gently guide them toward relaxation. We slow down the torrent of worries, we release the pinched-up muscles, and we stop struggling to accomplish impossible goals.

The way we create unhappiness is simple: We sense a problem, begin to struggle with it, and this struggle amplifies the problem ten or a hundred or a thousandfold. Most distresses wouldn't be a big deal if we didn't magnify them, and some distresses are even stimulating. Emotional upsets are like salt and pepper. Salt and pepper would taste terrible if we ate them with a spoon, but a sprinkle here and there adds zest and intensity.

If you consume emotional tension as a staple rather than as a seasoning, watch out for the attitude of straining—trying to force every situation to turn out "right." Straining involves pushing and struggling, as if mental exertion could solve our problems. ("Things go better with tension.") Straining is the worst of diseases, because it masquerades as a cure.

Strain is nearly always superfluous. All that's really going on in life is that we're sitting, talking, walking, reading, looking, laboring, loving—and experiencing what it feels like to do these simple things. Doing and being: The simplicity behind the complexity behind the simplicity.

The Basic Repertoire

Here is a summary of ten important methods described in the book. (For a list of all thirty techniques, see Appendix A.) Be sure to select at least one of the techniques from *Feel Better Now* and become thoroughly familiar with it, so you can use it effortlessly in a crisis situation.

Chapter One

Take a Breather. Enjoy a three-minute "time out" in which you breathe slowly, softly, and deeply. Imagine your stresses draining away with each long, leisurely exhalation.

Chapter Two

Think Soft. Locate a place where your body is tense. Imagine the tension turning into something soft, such as melting candle wax. Other images may be found in Chapter Two.

Word Magic. Repeat a word or phrase that encourages you to let go, such as "deeper and deeper peace."

Chapter Three

Twelve-Point Tension Release. Use the routine described in Chapter Three to relax your eyes, jaw, neck, shoulders, wrists, hands, torso, spine, buttocks, calves, ankles, and feet.

Body Release.

1. Locate the tensest muscles in your body and experience them, without necessarily trying to relax them.
2. Take a moment to feel how much energy you're expending to keep these muscles tight.
3. Imagine them becoming soft and pliable, as if they're turning into clay or warm candle wax.

Chapter Four

Changing Demands into Preferences. When you're feeling dissatisfied, identify the demand at the core of the unhappy feeling. Ask yourself, "What do I think I *have* to have in order to be happier?" Realize that it's fine to *prefer* whatever you like, but *demanding* it may be making you tense. Allow the demand to soften into a preference, and then do whatever you can to fulfill that preference.

Chapter Five

The Method of Choice.

1. Experience yourself straining, creating unpleasant feelings in your mind and body.
2. Ask yourself, "Am I willing to let go of straining?" Listen for an answer.
3. If the answer is yes, make a clear and conscious choice to let go.

Chapter Eight

Your Special Assets. Make a list of your own strengths and virtues, and carry it with you. When you're feeling low, pull out the list and spend a few minutes focusing on your strengths and thinking of examples of each one.

Chapter Ten

Opening Up to Pleasure.

1. Notice the feelings of pleasure you're experiencing.

2. Notice any tension that undermines the pleasure.
3. Let go and allow the good feelings to expand.

Chapter Thirteen

Spiritual Reconnection. Take a moment to reconnect with something larger than yourself—God, nature, your family, your religious community, or all of humanity.

Keeping the Balance

No system of personal growth is perfect for every person in every situation. Furthermore, it's possible to carry any good idea to an extreme, with peculiar results. This book is not meant as a panacea, but rather as a set of tools with both uses and limitations. Here are some possible limitations and criticisms of *Feel Better Now*.

1. Any self-help program can become a "should," so that we feel guilty when we don't carry it out. "I read a book about handling my upsets," we may think, "but today I feel angry. What's wrong with me?" None of us are perfect in the way we cope with stresses, and it's fine if we sometimes let little pressures get to us. At any given moment, a moderate amount of distress is not especially harmful. Our goal is *to reduce the percentage of our lives* that we spend in a state of useless upset. As long as we're making progress in that direction, specific moments of tension don't matter very much.
2. Because this book encourages us to notice our emotions, there is some danger of becoming preoccupied with every little twinge of distress. Worrying about the smallest signs of pushing, bracing, or straining is a waste of energy. Such "emotional hypochondria" can result from any approach that increases our awareness. Self-awareness is therapeutic, but even the best medicines have minor side effects. If a side effect becomes bothersome, one reduces the dosage.
3. Some people who read psychology books are searching for an anesthetic, a technique that would protect them from the tiniest pinpricks of emotional pain. This is probably neither possible nor desirable.

It's fine to accept the human mind as it is, with its full complement of responses. We can respect our nervous systems, even if they're a bit too nervous. We may be able to chuck out a lot of garbage and become happier human beings. But do we know so much that we can take a part of the mind and eliminate it? Shall we surgically remove the ability to be sad, mad, guilty, or anxious? Beware of attempting to remake human nature according to a "reasonable" blueprint.

So the ideas in this book could conceivably be distorted, exaggerated, or taken to an extreme, but in practice this is rare. We are more likely to underuse our tools for letting go, rather than to overuse them or misuse them.

A Choreography of the Heart

We're coming to the end of our work together as writer and reader. At this point it might be fitting for you to give yourself some credit for caring enough to finish the book. You did so because you want to drop some self-destructive mental habits and enrich your life. If you return to the beginning of *Feel Better Now* and read the first ten pages, you will find that your understanding of those pages has deepened. You may want to look through the book again at this new level of understanding. (Going over Chapter Six, the Mini-Manual, is especially useful.) Remember the value of *repetition* in learning ideas that the mind resists. And the mind certainly resists the notion that life could be a dozen times easier.

Other people will also resist this notion. Your friends haven't read the book or practiced its principles. If you tell them, "Why don't you just let go of that feeling?" they're likely to be irritated. They'll think you're discounting the significance of their own personal burdens.

Feel Better Now provides a pattern, a kind of mental choreography for coping with tensions and negative moods. As you interpret this choreography to fit your own style, remember that *you always have a choice* about how much you'll struggle with life and how much you'll simply let go and live it.

The temptation to struggle may be there for a long time. Our minds contain countless impulses directing us to do what's impossible. We want to change the unalterable past and to guarantee results in the unpredictable future. We want to have absolute security, and we imagine that if we "try hard enough" (make ourselves tense enough) we will get that security. To release this useless illusion opens the doorway to freedom.

Some people are afraid that happiness is impossible as long as their minds are presenting them with the same old movie-set of exaggerated hazards. Fortunately, this is not the case. Once you have mastered the art of letting go, you will continue to be aware of the creaks and clunks in your own mental machinery—but you will no longer take them so seriously. You will feel peaceful and self-confident as you observe the endless parade of challenges that passes in front of every human being on the planet.

It's better to dance with the mind than to fight with it. When you find yourself in a struggle, remember that you *do* know how to dance.

APPENDIX A:
List of Techniques for Reducing Stress

APPENDIX B:
Relaxers, Distracters, and Releasers
(See Chapter One for information about these three categories.)

Relaxers

Distracters

Releasers

Bibliography

On letting go:

Benson, Herbert, M.D., *The Relaxation Response*. New York: Avon Books, 1975.

Carrington, Patricia, Ph.D., *Releasing*. New York: William Morrow and Company, 1984.

On personal and spiritual growth:

Berne, Eric, M.D., *What Do You Say After You Say Hello?* New York: Bantam Books, 1972.

Ellis, Albert, Ph.D. and Knaus, William J., Ed.D., *Overcoming Procrastination*. New York: Institute for Rational Living, 1977.

Gelb, Michael J., *Present Yourself!* Rolling Hills Estates, California: Jalmar Press, 1988.

Haynes-Klassen, Joanne, *Learning to Live, Learning to Love*. Rolling Hills Estates, California: Jalmar Press, 1985.

Keyes, Ken, Jr., *Handbook to Higher Consciousness*. Berkeley, California: Living Love Center, 1974.

Keyes, Ken, Jr., Penny Keyes, and Staff, *Gathering Power Through Insight and Love*. Coos Bay, Oregon: Living Love Publications, 1987.

Macy, Joanna Rogers, Ph.D., *Despair and Personal Power in the Nuclear Age*. Philadelphia: New Society Publishers, 1983.

Maltz, Maxwell, M.D., *Psycho-Cybernetics*. New York: Pocket Books, 1960.

Parker, William R., Ph.D., *Prayer Can Change Your Life*. Englewood Cliffs, New Jersey: Prentice-Hall, 1957.

Rogers, Carl, Ph.D., *On Becoming a Person*. Boston: Houghton Mifflin Company, 1961.

Schriner, Chris, M.S., Rel.D., *Feeling Great*. Peoria, Illinois: Wesley-Kolbe Publishing Company, 1986.*

Schuller, Rev. Robert, *Believe in the God Who Believes in You*. Nashville, Tennessee: Thomas Nelson, 1989.

Selye, Hans, M.D., *The Stress of Life*. New York: McGraw-Hill Book Company, 1956.

Sparks, Ada, *The Two Minute Lover*. Rolling Hills Estates, California: Jalmar Press, 1989.

Stevens, John O., *Awareness: exploring experimenting experiencing*. Lafayette, California: Real People Press, 1971.

Tavris, Carol, Ph.D., *Anger: The Misunderstood Emotion*. Beaverton, Oregon: Touchstone Press, 1984.

Vitale, Barbara Meister, M.S., *Free Flight*. Rolling Hills Estates, California: Jalmar Press, 1986.

Special Note: Several personal growth seminars were mentioned in the Acknowledgements section just before the Table of Contents. Out of all of these, the Sedona Method is especially valuable for those who want to let go of upsets rapidly and directly. With practice, it works within seconds. The Sedona Method is available in several cities. Contact the Sedona Institute, 1645 E. Missouri, Suite 110, Phoenix, Arizona 85016, (602) 264-0123.

*Ordering information for *Feeling Great* — send $7.95 payable to Chris Schriner. Address: Living Arts, P. O. Box 3939, Costa Mesa, California, 92628-3939

About the Author

Dr. Chris Schriner is a psychotherapist with over twenty years of experience. He specializes in teaching people to handle stress *as it happens*, rapidly and directly. His workshops and lectures are offered at Orange Coast College, the Unitarian Universalist Fellowship of Laguna Beach, Orange Coast Unitarian Universalist Church, and other Southern California locations. Dr. Schriner has studied pastoral psychotherapy, and is state-licensed as a Marriage, Family and Child Counselor. In addition, he has completed human potential programs such as est, Lifespring, the Sedona Method, the Silva Method, and the Heller Method. His previous publications include *Feeling Great* and *Easy Effort*.

Openmind/Wholemind
Parenting & Teaching Tomorrow's Children Today

A book of powerful possibilities that honors the capacities, capabilities, and potentials of adult and child alike. Uses Modalities, Intelligences, Styles and Creativity to explore how the brain-mind system acquires, processes and expresses experience. Foreword by M. McClaren & C. Charles.
0-915190-45-1 $14.95
7 × 9   paperback
81 B/W photos 29 illus.

Present Yourself! *Captivate Your Audience With Great Presentation Skills*

Become a presenter who is a dynamic part of the message. Learn about Transforming Fear, Knowing Your Audience, Setting The Stage, Making Them Remember and much more. Essential reading for anyone interested in the art of communica-tion. Destined to become the standard work in its field.
0-915190-51-6   paper $9.95
0-915190-50-8   cloth $18.95
6 × 9   paper/cloth. illus.

Unicorns Are Real
A Right-Brained Approach to Learning

Over 100,000 sold. The long-awaited "right hemispheric" teaching strategies developed by popular educational specialist Barbara Vitale are now available. Hemispheric dominance screening instrument included.
0-915190-35-4 $12.95
8½ × 11   paperback, illus.

Unicorns Are Real Poster

Beautifully-illustrated. Guaranteed to capture the fancy of young and old alike. Perfect gift for unicorn lovers, right-brained thinkers and all those who know how to dream. For classroom, office or home display.
JP9027 $4.95
19 × 27   full color

Metaphoric Mind (Revised Ed.)

Here is a plea for a balanced way of thinking and being in a culture that stands on the knife-edge between catastrophe and transformation. The metaphoric mind is asking again, quietly but insistently, for equilibrium. For, after all, equilibrium is the way of nature.
0-915190-68-0 $14.95
7 x 10 paperback, B/W photos

Don't Push Me, I'm Learning as Fast as I Can

Barbara Vitale presents some remarkable insights on the physical growth stages of children and how these stages affect a child's ability, not only to learn, but to function in the classroom.
JP9112 $12.95
Audio Cassette

Tapping Our Untapped Potential

This Barbara Vitale tape gives new insights on how you process information. Will help you develop strategies for improving memory, fighting stress and organizing your personal and professional activities.

JP9111 $12.95
Audio Cassette

Free Flight *Celebrating Your Right Brain*

Journey with Barbara Vitale, from her uncertain childhood perceptions of being "different" to the acceptance and adult celebration of that difference. A book for right-brained people in a left-brained world. Foreword by Bob Samples.
0-915190-44-3 $8.95
5½ × 8½   paperback, illus.

"He Hit Me Back First"
Self-Esteem through Self-Discipline

Simple techniques for guiding children toward self-correcting behavior as they become aware of choice and their own inner authority.
0-915190-36-2 $12.95
8½ × 11   paperback, illus.

Learning To Live, Learning To Love

An inspirational message about the importance of love in everything we do. Beautifully told through words and pictures. Ageless and timeless.
0-915190-38-9 $7.95
6 × 9   paperback, illus.

Pajamas Don't Matter:
(or What Your Baby Really Needs)

Here's help for new parents everywhere! Provides valuable information and needed reassurances to new parents as they struggle through the frantic, but rewarding, first years of their child's life.
0-915190-21-4 $5.95
8½ × 11   paperback, full color

Why Does Santa Celebrate Christmas?

What do wisemen, shepherds and angels have to do with Santa, reindeer and elves? Explore this Christmas fantasy which ties all of the traditions of Christmas into one lovely poem for children of all ages.
0-915190-67-2 $12.95
8 1/2 x 11 hardcover, full color

Feelings Alphabet

Brand-new kind of alphabet book full of photos and word graphics that will delight readers of all ages.''. . .lively, candid. . .the 26 words of this pleasant book express experiences common to all children.''
Library Journal
0-935266-15-1 $7.95
6 × 9   paperback, B/W photos

The Parent Book

A functional and sensitive guide for parents who want to enjoy every minute of their child's growing years. Shows how to live with children in ways that encourage healthy emotional development. Ages 3-14.
0-915190-15-X $9.95
8½ × 11   paperback, illus.

Aliens In My Nest
SQUIB Meets The Teen Creature

Squib comes home from summer camp to find that his older brother, Andrew, has turned into a snarly, surly, defiant, and non-communicative adolescent. *Aliens* explores the effect of Andrew's new behavior on Squib and the entire family unit.
0-915190-49-4 $7.95
8½ × 11   paperback, illus.

Hugs & Shrugs
The Continuing Saga of SQUIB

Squib feels incomplete. He has lost a piece of himself. He searches every where only to discover that his missing piece has fallen in and not out. He becomes complete again once he discovers his own inner-peace.

0-915190-47-8 $7.95
8½ × 11   paperback, illus.

Moths & Mothers/
Feather & Fathers
A Story About a Tiny Owl Named SQUIB

Squib is a tiny owl who cannot fly. Neither can he understand his feelings. He must face the frustration, grief, fear, guilt and loneliness that we all must face at different times in our lives. Struggling with these feelings, he searches, at least, for understanding.

0-915190-57-5 $7.95
8½ × 11   paperback, illus.

Hoots & Toots & Hairy Brutes
The Continuing Adventures of SQUIB

Squib—who can only toot—sets out to learn how to give a mighty hoot. His attempts result in abject failure. Every reader who has struggled with life's limitations will recognize their own struggles and triumphs in the microcosm of Squib's forest world. A parable for all ages from 8 to 80.

0-915190-56-7 $7.95
8½ × 11   paperback, illus.

Do I Have To Go To School Today?
Squib Measures Up!

Squib dreads the daily task of going to school. In this volume, he daydreams about all the reasons he has not to go. But, in the end, Squib convinces himself to go to school because his teacher accepts him ''Just as he is!''

0-915190-62-1 $7.95
8½ × 11   paperback, illus.

The Turbulent Teens
Understanding Helping Surviving

"This book should be read by every parent of a teenager in America. . .It gives a parent the information needed to understand teenagers and guide them wisely.''—Dr. Fitzhugh Dodson, author of *How to Parent, How to Father,* and *How to Discipline with Love.*
0-913091-01-4 $8.95
6 × 9   paperback.

Learning The Skills of Peacemaking
An Activity Guide for Elementary-Age Children

"Global peace begins with you. Guide develops this fundamental concept in fifty lessons. If this curriculum was a required course in every elementary school in every country, we would see world peace in our children's lifetimes." — *Letty Cottin Pogrebin*, Ms. Magazine
0-915190-46-X $21.95
8½ × 11   paperback, illus.

Project Self-Esteem EXPANDED
A Parent Involvement Program for Elementary-Age Children

An innovative parent-support program that promotes children's self-worth. "Project Self Esteem is the most extensively tested and affordable drug and alcohol preventative program available."

0-915190-59-1 $39.95
8½ × 11   paperback, illus.

The Two Minute Lover
Announcing A New Idea In Loving Relationships

No one is foolish enough to imagine that s/he *automatically* deserves success. Yet, almost everyone thinks that they automatically deserve sudden and continuous success in marriage. Here's a book that helps make that belief a reality.
0-915190-52-4 $9.95
6 × 9   paperback, illus.

Reading, Writing and Rage

An autopsy of one profound school failure, disclosing the complex processes behind it and the secret rage that grew out of it.

Must reading for anyone working with learning disabled, functional illiterates, or juvenile delinquents.

0-915190-42-7 $12.95
5½ × 8½   paperback

Feel Better Now
30 Ways to Handle Frustrations in Three Minutes or Less

A practical menu of instant stress reduction techniques, designed to be used right in the middle of high-pressure situations. Feel Better Now includes stress management tools for every problem and every personality style.
0-915190-66-4 $9.95
6 × 9 paperback, appendix, biblio.

Esteem Builders

You CAN improve your students' behavior and achievement through building self-esteem. Here is a book packed with classroom-proven techniques, activities, and ideas you can immediately use in your own program or at home.

Ideas, ideas, ideas, for grades K-8 and parents.

0-915190-53-2 $39.95
8½ × 11   paperback, illus.

Good Morning Class—I Love You!
Thoughts and Questions About Teaching from the Heart

A book that helps create the possibility of having schools be places where students, teachers and principals get what every human being wants and needs—LOVE!

0-915190-58-3 $6.95
5½ × 8½ paperback, illus.

I am a blade of grass
A Breakthrough in Learning and Self-Esteem

Help your students become "lifetime learners," empowered with the confidence to make a positive difference in their world (without abandoning discipline or sacrificing essential skill and content acquisition).
0-915190-54-0 $14.95
6 × 9   paperback, illus.

Unlocking Doors to Self-Esteem

Presents innovative ideas to make the secondary classroom a more positive learning experience—socially and emotionally—for students and teachers. Over 100 lesson plans included. Designed for easy infusion into curriculum. Gr. 7-12

0-915190-60-5 $16.95
6 × 9 paperback, illus

SAGE: *Self-Awareness Growth Experiences*

A veritable treasure trove of activities and strategies promoting positive behavior and meeting the personal/social needs of young people in grades 7-12. Organized around affective learning goals and objectives. Over 150 activities.
0-915190-61-3   **$16.95**
6 × 9 paperback, illus.

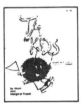